THE ANATOMY OF A COUPLES THERAPY SESSION

How does a couples therapist actually run a 50 minute session? What needs to happen? What must happen? Managing this time and knowing how to guide a couple through what can be a rocky roller coaster ride is a critical skill. This volume breaks down the entire 50 minutes of a couple's therapy session from beginning to end. It divides the 50 minutes into eight time period stages that may overlap. The distinctive characteristics and challenges of each time period are examined. Numerous case examples are given throughout the book. The couples therapist is addressed directly with many suggestions given for handling the situations that can arise in each period. In addition, the couples therapist's own experiences during the session are explored.

Judith P. Leavitt, EdD, is a senior clinician, licensed psychologist, and Diplomate Certified Sex Therapist with over 35 years of clinical experience. She has a private practice in Wayland, Massachusetts, where she works with individuals, couples, and families. At the William James College, a graduate college in psychology in Newton, Massachusetts, she is an adjunct faculty, teaching couples therapy and human sexuality.

THE ANATOMY OF A COUPLES THERAPY SESSION

The 50 Minute Hour in Eight Stages

Judith P. Leavitt, Ed.D.

Routledge
Taylor & Francis Group
NEW YORK AND LONDON

First published 2018
by Routledge
711 Third Avenue, New York, NY 10017

and by Routledge
2 Park Square, Milton Park, Abingdon, Oxon, OX14 4RN

Routledge is an imprint of the Taylor & Francis Group, an informa business

Library of Congress Cataloging-in-Publication Data
A catalog record for this book has been requested

ISBN: 978-1-138-06833-9 (hbk)
ISBN: 978-1-138-06834-6 (pbk)
ISBN: 978-1-315-15804-4 (ebk)

Typeset in Caslon Pro
by Keystroke, Neville Lodge, Tettenhall, Wolverhampton

Dedication

To my high school teacher Janet Jacobs who was the first person to give me confidence in my ability to write.

Contents

Acknowledgments

A deep thanks to Dean Abby and Alan Dodge Beck of William James College, both of whom gave me the opportunity to develop my ideas about working with couples through teaching couples therapy.

Special thanks to my editor George Zimmar for believing in this book.

I also want to acknowledge the great support of my partner, George Hecker, through my writing process. He helped me with his input, support, patience, and insights.

And a profound thanks to all the couples with whom I have worked over the years. You have been and continue to be my teachers.

INTRODUCTION

As I sit there waiting for Lena and Derek to come in, I wonder what is in store for me. Will they be yelling at each other? Will they be in a deep freeze? Will the room start to feel like the air has been sucked out of it? Will one of their children have acted up? Will one of their parents have become sick? And what of Derek's job issues that permeate the relationship? Will we be able to continue with last week's session? Will we build on skills that they are developing? Will we delve into one of the deeper issues in their relationship? I may have a plan for how the session is going to go. Yet anyone who has done couples therapy knows how quickly a plan may be scuttled. Anyone who has done couples therapy knows how even in the middle of the session everything can turn upside down. Doing couples therapy can be similar to a jazz improvisation. It is at once creative, exciting, unknown. It is building on themes, familiar tunes, and well-trained structures. At the same time, at any given moment a session can fall apart and not work. One must be flexible, quick, focused, and on top of one's game.

Much has been written about how to do couples therapy. There are many schools of thought and approaches, such as structural/strategic family therapy, narrative therapy, behavioral therapy, etc. In my graduate couples therapy class I teach many of these approaches. I am able to find many references for students to gain understanding of the issues and complexities of this work. The one thing I cannot find are specific references about the anatomy of a couples therapy session. *How does one run an actual session?* There are books on how to do an assessment, how to give feedback, how to work on communication, how to handle specific issues. Many couples therapy approaches present steps and exercises to be used in the course of couples therapy. However, there is *not* material available focused on the specific 50 minutes of an actual session. In case studies, authors sometimes describe a particular session and may give actual dialogue from that specific session. These sessions most often show only a part of a session—usually the most "significant" part. They illustrate the application of a specific theoretical approach and/or technique. But rarely do they describe the whole session from beginning to end, thus showing the different phases of the session and the important transitions from one phase to the next. Yet, there is a great deal of rich material to be explored about what takes place during the confines of a specific whole session. Running a couples therapy session can feel like a marvelous dance, a dreadful encounter, an opportunity for total failure. It can feel like jumping off a cliff and flying or crashing.

Writing this book was a joy. Often as I was working on a section, I would look over the couples sessions I had had that week. Material would pour out as I thought about what had happened. This was particularly true when I was working on certain sections, such as the different types of sessions described in Section V, Full Steam Ahead. Suddenly I would realize that a session I had run that week was a whole different type of session than those that I had described to date. It was exciting as it seemed like the material was limitless. I could then hardly wait for new sessions to occur so I could see if these sessions gave me yet more new material. There are undoubtedly types of sessions that will occur to you as readers as you go through this book. I invite you to add to the lists of ideas here.

My writing experience reinforced how creative couples therapy can be. Writing this book was a lot like doing a couples session: exciting, fun, playful, serious, challenging, and demanding, i.e. an experience with a full range of feelings.

Doing couples therapy demands that we as therapists be in the moment. There is a great deal that is happening right there in the room. A skilled couples therapist needs to absorb all that is happening, mix it in with his or her skills, handle often intense emotions, and find a helpful direction. This work can be among the most electrifying and challenging types of therapy a therapist can do. At the heart of the work is the session that is happening right now.

Too often I have had couples describe prior couples therapy in the following ways: the therapist just sat there, the therapist seemed disorganized, and/or the therapist did not seem to have control of the session. Recognizing that clients' reports on therapists may say more about the clients than the therapist, it is also true that during a couples therapy session it is easy for the therapist to become overwhelmed and lost. Couples therapy requires a great deal of skill. For the couples therapy to be effective, the couples therapist must be fully present and at the top of his or her game. Even then things can go awry.

The approach to couples therapy in this book is based primarily on an eclectic approach of structural/strategic, gestalt, systemic, behavioral, existential, multicultural, and psychodynamic therapies. Most couples therapists have an integrated approach of different backgrounds because a sole approach can be too limiting. The approach presented here is an active one in which the therapist is involved in the session, often jumping in, suggesting, guiding, educating, and taking control, as well as listening, responding, collaborating, supporting, and empathizing. This approach takes the position that clients come to therapists because of their training, skill, and expertise. They need to use these assets to best help the couple. Couples therapy is challenging and often difficult. It can easily lose focus, get lost, get out of control, and/or be harmful. Sometimes the description of the therapist's work can make it sound manipulative. For example, later in the book there is a discussion of the "setup" for a session. It is, in fact, necessary for the therapist to pay close attention to what is happening, direct traffic, interrupt, stop what is happening, redirect, position the partners to be ready for what may take place, etc. A good couples therapist needs to be unafraid to take control. A good couples therapist needs to be in charge of what is happening in order to make the therapy safe for the couple. Couples therapists cannot be merely reflective and supportive. Weeks et al. (2005) write, " For (couples) therapy to have the best chance to succeed the therapist must be in charge of how it proceeds . . ." (p. 22). They later write, "Maintaining control over structure and process cannot be emphasized enough. It is essential to secure control at the beginning of therapy or the couple will enact the same patterns that brought them to treatment" (p. 50).

Strategic, structural, and cognitive behavioral couples therapies share a focus on present events. They advocate that changing behavior in and of itself can produce significant change in people's lives. These therapies also look at the communication patterns between couples. Issues such as blaming, dismissing, negating, distancing, and interrupting set up dysfunctional communication patterns that can lead to serious relationship breakdowns such as lying, shutting down, and undermining. The couples therapist helps couples to see the communication patterns that develop between the partners. These patterns in strategic and structural therapies are described as sequences. According to Keim and Lappin (2002) a sequence is "a self-perpetuating interactional pattern also known as a transactional pattern" (p. 92).

The therapist points out the negative consequences of these patterns and suggests alternative interactions to improve the relationship. "The most practical way to help clients resolve marital problems is through active observation of, consideration of, and intervention in the client social system" (p. 87). Interventions in structural couples therapy include joining with the couple to create an alliance, observing an interaction pattern in the room, and developing interventions to change the couple dynamics (Greenan and Tunnell, 2003). Structured techniques are used to, help "a client experience, think, and/or behave differently" (Keim and Lappin, 2002, p. 102).

Baucom et al. (2015) write of Behavioral Couples Therapy (BCT), "The traditional BCT model also posits that a couple's relationship consists of reciprocal and circular sequences in which each partner's behavior simultaneously affects and influences that of the other" (p. 24). Cognitive behavioral therapy looks at cognitive patterns such as assumptions, attributions, selective attention, expectancies, and standards that lead to negative behavioral patterns between partners (Baucom et al., 2002). As partners begin to recognize these patterns and learn how to alter their behaviors, the relationship can markedly improve. The therapist's work is to point out these patterns and provide behavioral interventions to create new more functional patterns of interaction. As one example, behavioral therapy looks at couples developing behavioral contracts, known as contingency contracts. Thus, in a couple one partner might agree to invite the other for a date night to show that they do indeed value spending time together.

Structural therapy (Keim and Lappin, 2002) focuses on the structures that couples (and families) create in their relationships. Structures that are examined include: hierarchies of power, roles, triangulations, boundaries, and coalitions. These structures can create dysfunctions and cause distress, tensions, and distance in relationships. Altering the structures can significantly change how couples interact and feel in the relationship. For example, if one partner controls the household, changing some of the responsibilities in the relationship can help to rebalance the couple.

Underlying these approaches to couples therapy is systemic therapy which looks at the couple's relationship as a system made up of many parts. The parts are like gears that interact, allowing the relationship to function. When a gear is not working, when two or more gears are not meshing, when there is not the proper lubrication of the gears, the system and the parts of the system can break down. Systemic couples therapy looks at the many elements that make up a couple and the interaction between these elements. Issues such as age, culture, level of commitment, family background, health, job situation, children, religion, and many more all play important roles in the couple's relationship. Integrative approaches such as Emotionally Focused Couples Therapy (Johnson, 2015) incorporate many of these systemic and behavioral approaches.

Phenomenological psychology is described by Spinelli (1989) as the study of an individual's conscious experience of the world. This approach recognizes that each person is unique and perceives the world in his or her own way. Phenomenological psychology is concerned with understanding the relativity of each person's perceptions and meanings (Brazier, 1993). In phenomenological therapy, the therapist helps clients to examine, clarify, and understand their perceptions and meanings in order to gain more mastery and control in their lives. The focus is on immediate experience. Spinelli (1989) writes "the therapy places strong emphasis on the immediate here and now experience of both the client and the therapist" (p. 130). Mindfulness as a practice that informs therapeutic work shares this emphasis on immediate experience (Germer and Siegel, 2013).

Gestalt therapy as developed by Fritz and Laura Perls (1969) was influenced strongly by phenomenological psychology as well as Zen Buddhism. Perls's therapy work focused on the immediate experience of the clients by looking at their feelings and sensations. The gestalt therapist intervenes to help clients gain greater awareness of how their perceptions lead to their concept of reality. The focus in the therapy session is on what is happening now. Cognitive behavioral therapy has a common base with phenomenological psychology. Both emphasize perceptions and the creation of meaning in the client experience. They focus on the client's view of reality. Spinelli (1989) writes of behaviorism and phenomenological psychology "both . . . focus upon observation and description" (p. 173). Thus strategic and structural therapies, phenomenological psychology, and cognitive behavioral therapy work together and share many basic tenets. They are the foundation of the couples therapy approach in this book.

The theories upon which this book is based are distinctly Western. They were developed by psychologists, therapists, and philosophers from the Western world. Yet some of the approaches, such as phenomenology, as mentioned, are influenced by philosophies from the Eastern world. We are seeing the growing influence of mindfulness in psychology and psychotherapy (Germer and Siegel, 2013). The focus on what is happening right in the room is very similar to mindfulness. The couples therapist is using all his or her senses and observation skills to attend to what is happening right now in the session.

How does one apply the training one has as a couples therapist to couples from other cultures, couples who may think differently, and have different values than you as a Western-trained couples therapist? More and more couples therapists are presented with couples from India, Pakistan, Puerto Rico, Haiti, Russia, etc. In addition, we have more couples of mixed backgrounds, for example a Caucasian American wife and a Chinese husband. Thus, doing this work requires a multicultural approach. What does this involve? Hardy and Laszloffy (2002) in their article "Couple Therapy Using a Multicultural Perspective" give basic principles of a multicultural approach to couples therapy. This list includes such principles as understanding how the partners make meaning in their lives, how the couple negotiates differences, and what cultural legacies and loyalties each partner brings to the couple relationship. Throughout this book issues of cultural difference will be discussed since they make a notable impact upon the couples therapy.

The purpose of this book is to help therapists to grapple with the 50 minutes in front of them in a couples therapy session. The book will look at the following issues: the structure of a session, the purpose of a session, how to begin the session, where to go during the session, timing during a session, the different types of sessions, and finishing the session. Throughout the book examples of sessions will be given from published case studies. These examples show specific aspects of what goes on in a session. Yet rarely are these examples set in the context of the whole session—the whole 50 minutes.

This book will also address the therapist's experiences during the 50 minutes as these experiences play an important role in how the session works. Too often as therapists we look only at what is going on with our couple and we don't see what is going on within us. Couples therapy profoundly affects us. It may lift us up or bring us down. It may excite us, giving us a strong sense of making a difference in people's lives. Likewise, doing couples therapy can make us question our competence and ability to do anything useful as a therapist. A couples session gone wrong can be devastating. So much happens in a couples session that there is ample opportunity for us to doubt ourselves and double-think what we are doing. This work is not for the faint of heart. We can easily feel out of control when we have two people in front of us hurling insults back and forth at each other at high volume. We are witness to some of the most profound hurt, disappointment, and betrayal in human relationships. Some days we walk out of our offices shaking our heads, asking ourselves how can people who love each other be so cruel and why did we get into this work? Other days we walk out uplifted by the power of caring, healing, perseverance, and courage to which we are witness.

Couples watch us carefully. It can be so surprising when a partner says something like, "You often sigh when you are fed up with us." In reaction you may think, "What? She was watching me that closely? I thought they were so caught up in each other that they did not notice what I was doing." Our experiences can be read by the couple and can influence the session. If you are bored, it may affect the motivation of the couple. If you are annoyed, your tone may put off the partner you are confronting. If you are moved, your compassion may help to open up a partner's emotions. It is easy to get so caught up in handling the session, that you miss how you are feeling and how that may be coming through to the couple.

Summary of the Time Frames of a Session

A couples therapist needs to be very sensitive to aspects of the structure of the session. Each session has its own arc. These arcs vary enormously. Clearly there is a beginning and an end, both of which need to be attended to carefully. Many sessions have a critical point during which the session's direction is determined. Hopefully this occurs towards the beginning of the session, allowing for enough time for the unfolding of the direction. However, sometimes the direction does not become clear until well into the session or even towards the end. Sometimes the direction of the session changes, creating another beginning. What has gone on before usually, but not always, influences what takes place after the change in direction. Another factor impacting the structure of the session is the speed of the session. How quickly are things happening? There are slow sessions, there are fast sessions, and there are sessions whose speed varies up and down during the session.

In conducting a couples therapy session, it is important to have a clock easily visible. As the therapist you need to check the clock often to see how much time you have left. For example, if a brand new loaded topic arises with ten minutes left, it is probably wise to defer the topic to another session. As the therapist you need to be able to see the clock announcing that you have ten minutes left. Hopefully you are able to look at the clock without it being obvious to the couple, although at times you may need to tell the couple what the timing is. In the above example you might want to say, "We have ten minutes left, so let's hold on to this charged topic until next time."

In this book the 50 minutes of a couples therapy session are divided into time frames. The time frames for each section overlap with each other because rarely is a couple session neatly divided into the sections given below. These divisions are given because they often do occur during a couple session. However, couples therapy sessions can be anything but neat and clear-cut. The time frames may differ greatly. In any given session some of these time frames don't happen, or the time frames may not be in order, or in the middle of one time frame another may appear. Even though there is order, couples therapy is also an improvisation.

The first time frame discussed is the Lead-in. What happens as the session approaches? The Lead-in may include couple interactions well before the session, on the way to the session, sitting in the waiting room, first interacting with you the therapist, entering the office and settling into the session.

The next time frame is the Beginning: the first 5 minutes. How do you get a session going? This section looks at issues such as structured and open-ended beginnings, the importance of connecting with your couple, your experiences as the therapist, and "bad beginnings."

The third time frame is Finding Direction: 5–10 minutes. This is the time that a clear direction for the session is usually set. This section looks at the many issues in establishing a direction. Examples include: is the direction a safe direction, is it a workable direction, how do you recognize rumblings that may indicate an important direction, and what do you do when the session is floundering?

The fourth time frame is Establishing the Work: 10–20 minutes. A direction is chosen. Now how do you get where you want to go? This is the period for laying the ground work for the direction chosen. It involves setting up the work and establishing the parameters within which the work will unfold. Issues such as when is the work likely to be productive, when is it trouble, and when is it unproductive are discussed.

The fifth time frame is Full Steam Ahead: 15–40 minutes. Now comes the period in which the body of the work is actually done! An analogy is taking a trip. The Getting Underway period is figuring out where you are going. Establishing the Work is pouring over maps, getting suitcases, loading the car, and starting on your way. Full Steam Ahead is the actual trip with its detours, stops, change of drivers, arguments, singing in the car, etc. This particular section examines 26 different specific types of sessions that can take place. These 26 are divided into four categories of sessions: Difficult Couples Therapy Sessions, Classic Couples Therapy Sessions, Special Types of Couples Therapy Sessions, and Deeper Couples Therapy Sessions. In addition, intervention exercises, often a staple of couple therapy, are discussed.

The sixth time frame is Pulling It Together: 35–45 minutes. You have 10 to 15 minutes left to go in the session. This is the time to bring things together. What has just happened? What has the couple learned? What needs to be said and done before the session is over? This is the time for "ahas" to occur. Different types of ahas and steps for helping couples come to aha moments are discussed. Likewise, obstacles to being able to pull the session together are also explored.

Finally, there is the Ending: 45–50 minutes. It is time for the work to be finished and for the couple to go on their way. During this time you as the therapist may give a summary of the session, assign homework, and/or help the couple with a transition back to their day. Payment and scheduling may be addressed; challenging issues, such as handling post-session effects, are discussed.

There is yet one more time frame: Leaving. This is the post-session time in which the couple gets up, finishes any business at hand, and walks out of the office. Much can still happen during these few minutes. Different types of leavings such as reluctant leavings, abrupt leavings, and awkward leavings are discussed.

Throughout the book, examples from written case studies are used. Many case studies give a description of phases of the therapy or of the progress of the therapy overall. These cases are not useful for this book because they do not describe specific sessions. In addition, written cases are usually used to illustrate a specific approach to couples therapy, such as cognitive behavioral or object relations. The cases referred to in this book describe specific sessions, showing what actually happened in those sessions. Even these cases rarely describe certain phases of the sessions such as the Lead-in, the Beginning, the Ending, and the Leaving. They focus primarily on the main body of the work of the session. This occurs during the Full Steam Ahead time frame from 15–40 minutes. This is when the meat of the work is done, making it seemingly the most important time in the session. Yet what takes place during the Lead-in, the Beginning, the Ending, etc. is of utmost importance for the success of the session. These periods are neglected in the literature. Yet, anyone who does couples therapy knows how critical they are to the whole session. They clearly exist and they provide the framework for what happens. This book was written to flesh out the whole session from beginning to end.

Section I
The Lead-in

1
Starting Off

The session has started before it begins! You can smell the smoke coming from the smoldering partners in your waiting room. Issues from the prior session may still be stewing. Or you may get a startling email about the upcoming session. This is the Lead-in period to a session. There are many ways the Lead-in can happen. There are also many places where and times when it can happen.

The couple may start the session on the ride over to the appointment. They may talk about what they want to discuss in the session. They may break into an argument in the car. They may hash over an event that has occurred that day. If the partners came separately, they may have talked over their cell phones on the way there. There may be tension, electricity, and/or exasperation that the couple brings into the session fresh from immediately before the session.

Minuchin and Nichols (1998) recount a lead-in to a session in which the couple was 25 minutes late. In addition, the husband arrived first and said that while the couple was waiting for a subway, his wife suddenly decided to take a cab by herself. Right away it is evident that something was up; something not good. In a later session the wife got lost on the way to the office after being there three times before. This provided a lead-in to a discussion of her helplessness.

Then there is the waiting room and walking into a session. As the therapist, you need to have antennae out upon first contact with the couple. If you sit near your waiting room, you may hear that loud silence right outside your door. Right away you need to be alert for what this silence is about. Perhaps they are in the middle of a cold standoff. Perhaps one of them is ready to pounce as soon as he/she walks into the room. He/she is just waiting for you to be present. Or perhaps the couple is just quietly reading magazines. Shapiro (2010) describes the waiting room behavior of a couple in a case study. In his description aspects of the differences in the partner's behavioral styles are evident. The husband is "very organized and calm" whereas the wife rushes in "talking on her cell phone while precariously balancing coffee for both" (p. 407). When you walk out to call a couple for a session, you need to do a quick scan for information: where is each partner sitting, what is each wearing, what are their expressions, how are they interacting, and what is their affect? Next, it is important to take in how each greets (or doesn't greet) you.

Then comes the walk into your office, the small talk, or lack of it and the sitting down. What kind of energy does each person have when entering the room? What contact do the partners have with each other as they come in? Where do they sit? What facial expressions and posture do they exhibit? How do they interact with you the therapist? If there are choices about where to sit, the couple may debate about who sits where. This can be playful or hostile. It is particularly helpful to notice any inconsistencies you see compared to what you have observed before. As examples of different entrances to the therapy room, Jed and Alicia fairly drag themselves into the office in silence whereas Martha and Beth burst in chattering away with each other about some incident in their life. Alicia, who is always dressed to the nines, comes in wearing sweats. Idelma enters into a chat with you ignoring her partner who slumps into the chair. Dickson et al. (2011) describe a couple as they come into the office as follows: "Mara and Richard seemed 'lighter' as they entered the therapy room. They were caught smiling at each other at times, with obvious warmth and affection" (p. 101).

If the couple is busily into a discussion with each other, it is important to hear whether it is about themselves or whether it is about something unrelated to the therapy. Sometimes you can glean some quick insight into who the partners are in their outside world by a conversation they are having, say about their work day or their children. One might be talking about being manipulated by a coworker and wanting to get back at this person. You may get a glimpse of a side of a partner that you do not see in the relationship.

One of the first decisions you need to make is whether to say something about what you are picking up on as the couple enters. For example, do you say, "Something seems to be going on. What's happening?" Or, "You're laughing today. Is this a good sign?" Or, "I could cut the tension in the room with a knife." This is part of a quick assessment. Already your mind is in high gear watching, assessing, preparing.

If there is nothing very obvious as a couple enters the room, how do you handle that time period as the couple settles in? Do you talk about the construction out front, the playoff game many people are talking about, the hurricane last week? You try to gauge what might be appropriate small talk to set the couple at ease, and/or to make a connection with the couple. Perhaps the situation calls for no small talk.

The Lead-in period has a characteristic that is similar to the Leaving period. It seems outside of the therapy session itself, therefore leaving an opening for "real world" concerns and interactions. For example, sometimes one partner will ask you a personal question. It might be something seemingly as simple as, "How are you?" How to answer this question may be straightforward or complex, depending on what the person is really asking. Usually a simple, "Fine, thanks" is sufficient. For example, after Thanksgiving a couple might ask you, "How was your Thanksgiving. Did you spend it with family?" Is it appropriate to say anything about this, such as, "Yes, we went to our daughter's house," or, "We spent a quiet Thanksgiving by ourselves?" Would it be better simply to say the usual, "Fine. How was yours?" The answer may vary with the couple. You need to assess how the answer is going to impact each individual, the couple, and potentially the session. Right away the issue of boundaries comes up.

"Have you ever been divorced?" Sometimes a partner will ask you about something more personal. A partner may want to know who you are beyond your role as a therapist in a way that would not be helpful. This could be flattering as this partner expresses an interest in you. If you have been sick, a partner may ask about how you are doing. How much do you share? What is appropriate? The couple may need to be put at ease as one or both may be concerned about their therapy being affected. One of the challenges of doing this work is at once developing a meaningful relationship with clients and at the same time not sharing inappropriately about your personal life.

Sometimes you may have to initiate a more personal discussion. You may need to tell the couple that you will be out for some personal reason. It could be medical or family-related. How much do you reveal? This depends upon the situation, the possible impact the information and your absence will have, how much they may know or will find out from other sources, whether the situation will touch on their experiences, and how you yourself are handling your situation. Sometimes what you have to say will be physically obvious to them because you are pregnant, have a bandage or a cast, etc. When some discussion has to take place, it is important to think about how to have it in the best possible way, a way that may even help the therapy and the couple. Unless the couple is in clear distress, it is generally best to have any of these discussions during this Lead-in time before the session itself begins. This allows there to be a distinction between the Lead-in and the Beginning of the session so that the Lead-in does not interfere with the session. Once this discussion is over, then you can signal that the session itself is beginning saying something such as, "Now let's focus on you." There certainly are times when this type of discussion blends into the Beginning of the session and the lines are not so clear. It is also helpful to have these types of discussions during the Lead-in rather than at the end of the session when too much could get stirred up without time to handle the concerns.

Sometimes there may, in fact, be a personal (or seemingly personal) connection between you and one or both of the partners. This could simply be that you have a relationship with one or both of their individual therapists. Or one partner may be in a group with another of your clients. It might be that during the therapy you discover that you know people in common. It is during the Lead-in time period that these connections are likely to come up. Of course, you need to be on the watch for any ethical boundaries and handle them appropriately. In general, when there are personal connections, you should be careful not to say a great deal. If there is to be discussion about a conversation you had with one of their individual therapists (with, of course, written releases of information), this must be carefully considered since what was said between therapists may not be appropriate to discuss, especially with the other partner in the room. Usually it is helpful simply to acknowledge that a discussion took place and was helpful. If more than a passing reference is made, it will likely become part of the Beginning of the session.

Some couples therapists prefer to do the business part of the therapy during the Lead-in time. They handle payments and scheduling before the session begins. Issues about these interactions are discussed in the Leaving period since many therapists handle these concerns at the end of the session. An advantage of dealing with these issues at the beginning is to get them over with and perhaps spend less time on them in order to get on with the session. One main disadvantage is that doing these transactions first may interfere with what is happening for the couple as they enter the room. In addition, they may emphasize the business aspect of the relationship rather than the personal connection between the therapist and the couple.

What do you do if one person is present and one person is going to be late? Do you start without the other person? Do you allow one person to be "present" by phone while driving? Do you tell the person present that you will wait until both partners are there to begin? Do you handle the situation differently depending on the reason that one person is not there yet? For example, what if the late person got stuck in an unexpected traffic jam? What if that partner is chronically late? It is important for you as the couples therapist to have a policy about how you proceed when one partner is late. Your client is the couple. Therefore most of the time it is advisable to wait to start until both people are present in the room. Sometimes one partner will just walk in and push to start without the other. You may then have to hold the boundary more firmly, creating tension before the session begins. If you do start without the other person, you can create an imbalance because the partner not present may feel excluded (even if it his/her own doing that he/she is late). There may be special circumstances in which you would start with one partner. If, for example, the partner present is worried about the other partner's absence and needs help from you in some way.

And what if one person shows up and the other is not able or willing to come? The person who shows up may say that they didn't want to waste the session or have to pay for the session, so he/she came alone. That partner may not have even learned that the other person isn't coming until he/she is sitting in the waiting room.

The clearest way to handle this situation is to explain at the first session that your client is the couple, that you do not see people individually by default, and that if you are going to see the partners individually, there needs to be a plan to do so. However, if you have not explained this, or even if you have, you may find yourself presented with only one partner in front of you. In certain circumstances, you may decide to go ahead and see that person if, for example, you think that you can help the couple by doing this.

To illustrate, Jake showed up by himself to the couples session. When you as the therapist came out into the waiting room, Jake explained that Ross would not be coming. They had had a big argument in which Ross had blown up and said mean things to Jake. Jake was miffed that Ross would not come and was concerned that he would not return to therapy. You wondered if Ross did not come out of embarrassment since he had been working on controlling his rages. You were also concerned about losing the couple. You thought that by hearing the situation and talking through with Jake how to handle the situation, you could possibly bring Ross back. In fact, you suggested that Ross come in by himself next time, thinking you could work with him about what was behind his blowing up. After the session Jake spoke about this with Ross who liked the idea of coming in by himself. Indeed, when Ross came in alone, he expressed that he felt deeply humiliated about his mean behavior. You were able to support Ross by showing him concern, and helping him to apologize to Jake. What came out of these two sessions allowed the couple to resume their therapy which otherwise might have ended.

The Lead-in time may be an important time with a couple from another culture. What if the couple is speaking in their own language in the waiting room? Now they must switch to English unless you speak their language. You may notice a difference in their affect right away. With some couples you might help them to feel comfortable by asking them about their language. You might ask them what a certain word in their language is, a word that relates to something happening such as the current very hot weather. Or you might ask them what the weather is like in their country right now. These segues, if appropriately done, can help the couple to feel more comfortable coming into your office. You need to be careful not to be patronizing.

If you are familiar with the couple's country/culture, you might establish an ongoing reference to their country, such that you could make reference to it as you enter the therapy room. For example, you might say something about a news item that involves their country.

The Therapist's Experiences

The Lead-in is a time of possibility. As a therapist you do not know what is going to happen. This is the time when your radar is looking out for clues. This can be an exciting time, a time of apprehension, a time of anxiety, and/or a time of fascination. What will happen? Will you be up for it? Will this be like other sessions after which you want to go home and curl up under a blanket? Or will this be a time of growth, opening, and breaking through? Will you feel blocked, determined, frustrated, challenged, competent, moved? It is important to notice your own feelings as you go into the session so that you know how they may play a role in the upcoming session. Many times the Lead-in is simple and uneventful. It is not likely to knock you off your pins. When it does, you had best get yourself strapped in for an intense session. You need to have a recovery plan in order to have a helpful Beginning.

Case Vignette

Ling and Henry left the last couple sessions hugging and close. However, today when you come out of your office, they are sitting in stony silence. Henry sits with legs planted apart, head leaning back against the wall. Ling sits crossed-legged with crossed arms and a scowl, and steam coming out of her head. In order to get to the water cooler to get some water, you need to walk between them. It feels like the space between Ling and Henry is dangerous territory.

After each barely gets out a hello, they walk into your office in silence and sit down. You look at one and then the other and take in a deep audible breath as a way to acknowledge the tension. Then you say, leaning toward them with concern, "I can feel the tension between you. Something has certainly shifted since the end of our last session. What is happening?"

Ling glowers. "It's bad." Henry rolls his eyes. Ling says, "I don't think I can do this anymore." This is a refrain for Ling when she is unhappy with Henry. You decide not to bite. You wait.

Henry says to Ling, "You go."

Ling snaps back, "No, you tell it." This is the first glimmer of some information. Something has happened. You decide to wait. You want the couple to work out how they are going to begin to get into the issues. Henry starts. Ling interrupts right away. "Tell the whole story," she says sarcastically. It's time for you to step in. You say, "I am interested to know what has happened that is causing this tension. How about, Henry, you say how you see it and then, Ling, you add your perspective." The session has begun.

Summary of the Lead-in

The Lead-in may include couple interactions well before the session, on the way to the session, sitting in the waiting room, first interacting with you the therapist, entering the office, and settling into the session. Situations such as a partner being late, a partner asking you a personal question, and handling payment are discussed.

Section II Beginning: The First 5 Minutes

2
Introduction and Open-ended or Structured Beginning

Take a deep breath. You are about to embark on a 50-minute unknown journey. How do you begin? These first few minutes are a time of gathering information and making a quick assessment of what is facing you today. There is usually an abundance of information for you to pick up in the first few minutes of the session. For example, as Paul sits down, he stares expectantly straight ahead at you. Red in the face, he folds his arms over his chest. Meanwhile, his wife has slumped down into the chair and stares at the floor. The tension is palpable. When you pick up such strong signals, you need to decide whether to pursue what is happening or to start the session in a different way. If you have seen this kind of behavior often with Paul and his wife, you may not want to engage with it.

Who starts the session? Most often you as the therapist begin. Two options for how to begin include an open-ended approach or a structured approach. Examples of an open-ended beginning include, "How are you doing, how are things going," or, "Where would you like to begin?" One advantage to this approach is that it allows the couple to bring up any burning issues. One of the most important things to determine at the beginning of the session is whether there have been significant couple events during the week. Has the couple had an important discussion during the week? Have they had an argument? Have they had a good experience together? Did somebody get drunk and embarrass the other? Did somebody break a promise or overstep a boundary? If they have had an argument during the week, or if a crisis has developed, an open-ended approach allows these issues to come up. This approach allows you to get more of a feel of where the couple is at this moment. You can watch to see what is going on for the couple right there in the room. An open-ended beginning also allows the couple to decide the direction they want to take.

Freedman and Combs (2015) describe a session in which the couple comes in with their own agenda. They describe one of their "awful fights" (p. 292) and what they had done to learn something from the fight.

How do you not get in the way of an important issue that the couple wants to raise? Couples therapists have all been in the situation in which a partner says, with 15 minutes left, "There is something important I wanted to talk about today." As the therapist you think, "What? Where did that come from? Why didn't that come up before? What did I miss?" However the session begins, you need to watch for signs that one or both of the partners are not connecting with what is happening. Is one of them distracted, anxious, overreactive etc.? Is one not fully participating? You may need to check in specifically with each partner and ask if there is something either of them wants to deal with that day.

When what has happened during the week becomes the focus of the session, you have the opportunity to work with fresh material and to intervene with suggestions that can make a difference right there in the room. If you begin the session with a structured approach, such as following through with homework, you may miss important events that have taken place between the couple during the week.

Yet these events can also be a distraction or a repetition of the couple's dynamics in a way that actually blocks the couple's progress. They can lead you on a wild goose chase. Thus, it is important for you to determine the significance of what has happened. Is it relevant to the issues that the couple is addressing in therapy? Does the couple want to talk about what has happened? Are they are even able to focus on anything else? Sometimes you may want to redirect the session away from the weekly events, but the couple is too immersed in what has happened.

Thus, at the beginning there can be a tension between dealing with what is happening now versus focusing on an ongoing issue. As the therapist, deciding between these two may be your first task of the session.

Sometimes you may learn about what has happened from an outside source. A common source is from an individual therapist used by one of the couple. When this happens, you need to decide whether to let the couple know that you know. On the one hand, it may affect how either member of the couple feels if he/she knows that you have learned about the events already. On the other hand, it can be awkward if it emerges that you have known, but you do not say so. It can be difficult for you to sit on the knowledge of something important, particularly if the couple doesn't raise the issue and if the couple engages in a discussion of something less significant or pressing.

When would you begin with a structured approach? Examples of a structured approach include, "I'd like to pick up where we left off in the last session", "I think today we need to focus on the issue of blaming," "Last week was an intense session, so I want to check in with you about the issues we discussed," "I've been thinking about your couple therapy and I'd like to make a suggestion for today."

An advantage to a structured approach is that it sets boundaries for the session. This may be particularly important with a couple that has difficulty focusing. High-conflict couples often need containment right from the start of the session. Other advantages to a structured approach are (1) it allows for working toward a specific goal, (2) it can teach important skills, (3) it can provide safety, (4) it puts you in charge, and (5) it provides follow-up, exercises, and possibly homework.

One type of structured approach for beginning the session is following through with homework. It may be important to start the session with input about the homework in order to keep continuity with the last session. Apfelbaum (1995) describes a case in which sessions often began with processing of structured homework assignments. The assignments were based upon Masters and Johnson's sensate focus work plus written reflections about the exercises. The processing of the homework also became the focus of the work that developed in the sessions.

Dickson et al. (2011) describe beginning couple sessions with a review of homework. One session in their case study begins with going over the couple's assignment to "compose a list of their current feelings and what they thought was contributing to them" (p. 99).

It may be difficult to follow through with homework if the couple is in the midst of other issues that are hard to interrupt. In the heat of the moment a therapist may decide not to focus on the homework. However, it is critical that sometime during the session the therapist acknowledge that the homework was not discussed. A pitfall for couples therapists is assigning homework and then not following through with what the couple has done. Sometimes couples complain that in prior couples therapy homework was not discussed.

Another type of structured beginning involves you giving a summary of what has happened in the last session or several sessions. Sometimes couples who have difficulty beginning a session or remembering the last sessions are helped by such a summary. A summary can also provide containment for the couple if it is needed. If the couple has not been in for a session for a while, it may be particularly helpful to start with a summary of their past sessions and an evaluation of where they are in the therapy. They may need to get reoriented and to evaluate what they want to do in their couple therapy. Sometimes even when a couple has been coming regularly, it is helpful for them to step back and evaluate their therapy.

A third type of structured beginning involves starting the session with an exercise. Although exercises are usually introduced later in the session (see the section on intervention exercises in the Full Steam Ahead period), there are times when it may be helpful to start right off the bat with an exercise. Beginning with an exercise can set the tone and/or direction for the session. This may be particularly helpful when (1) you are working with a high-conflict couple, (2) you are working with a couple who has difficulty getting started, or (3) you are teaching a couple important skills such as conflict resolution skills. Gollan et al. (2002) describe beginning a couples session by introducing "behavior exchange" activities which include, "Offering positive compliments, tracking each other's efforts, and expressing appreciations for each other" (p. 668).

In looking at structured beginnings an important question arises. Where does the responsibility lie for beginning a couples session? Does it lie with you the therapist, with the couple, or both? More particularly, where do you think the responsibility needs to lie for this current session with this couple? Perhaps you need to take charge. Or perhaps the couple needs to work out for themselves where they want the session to go. Most often, when a couple is well engaged there is a balance and good negotiation between the therapist and the couple. Sometimes, for example, you could ask a couple, "Would you like to start the sessions today or would you like me to start?"

Another type of structured beginning is the preemptive beginning. This involves you saying something that is intended to ward off or diffuse a situation. For example, acknowledging that one or both of the partners were unhappy with the last session may ward off the partners from being withdrawn or uncooperative. By bringing the feelings out and acknowledging them right away, you may help the partners to feel heard and to be more ready to move ahead today. As another example, you might say something like, "I know you may still be upset about money issues, but we said that today we were going to focus on how to enjoy your upcoming vacation. Shall we proceed with that agenda?"

Couples from some countries/cultures may expect you to begin the session because they see you as the authority, because they do not know how to begin, and/or because they feel unfamiliar with how therapy works and are looking to you for guidance. It is important to set such a couple at ease. An open-ended beginning may make an already uncomfortable situation even more uncomfortable. As the therapist you need to figure out how best to make the therapy session a safe place. Setting a structure that could enable the couple to participate fully is important. For example, there might be certain greeting rituals in the couple's background that you can observe. You may need to talk about non-therapy topics longer than you would normally. Then you may need to describe what the focus for the session will be so that the couple knows what to expect. When you have a couple from a different culture than your own, it is important to learn about that culture and some of its customs in order to be helpful to the couple.

The beginning of a session may be a hybrid of an open-ended approach and a structured approach. For example, you might do a quick check-in, asking how the partners are doing and then introduce a structure. The check-in is to see if anything is brewing. Then the structure is to introduce a possible specific direction. Hoyt (2015) recounts the beginning of a solution-focused couple therapy as follows: "I began Session 2 by asking, 'So how's the state of the union? What's better?' " (p. 325). Thus, he starts with an open-ended question and then sets a direction.

Case Vignette of a Structured Beginning

In the last couples therapy session Walker and Clarissa were in a heated disagreement about what activities to do during their sexual experiences. Clarissa had very specific ideas of how she wanted the two of them to play out her sado-masochistic sexual fantasies. Walker was trying to go along with Clarissa's desires, but he was getting tired of the roles she wanted him to play. He wanted to have a say in what they did. At the same time he was trying to make up to her for being judgmental about her fantasies in the past. The last session had started with them planning new ways of being sexual together. However, Walker's anger and Clarissa's defensiveness hijacked this effort and you as the couples therapist had shifted to addressing their conflict dynamic. Walker was spitting out resentment over Clarissa's control and Clarissa was glaring back at him as she defended her sexual desires. They were not happy with each other nor with the focus on their conflict dynamic. Yet, their conflict could not be ignored. In between the sessions, Walker called to cancel their therapy. Then Clarissa called to say that they had talked further and did want to continue. You asked them to come in with a clear agenda of what they wanted from the next session.

At the beginning of the next session you acknowledge what has happened and emphasize that you really want the therapy to work for them. You plan at some point in the session to talk about the importance of addressing their dynamic as part of the therapy. Yet you know that they need to have the control to (1) show that they can take charge of their therapy, and (2) direct the session to be what they want. Clarissa begins by saying that they have agreed that they want to combine her fantasies with some spontaneity in their sexual life. You can see that this is a concession on her part to Walker. Clarissa says they want to talk about starting a sexual experience with her S&M fantasy and then allow for some freer expression. She says they need help with this. You check with Walker about this direction for the session and Walker concurs. You are aware of the thin line you walk in supporting each partner, given the fragility of their agreement and their readiness to bolt from the therapy.

This case example shows yet another type of structured beginning. You as the couples therapist ask the couple to come in with a clear direction for the session because of the couple's ambivalence about returning to therapy. The session begins with you focusing on what the couple has discussed about what they want from the session. The structure is necessary to try to salvage the therapy. This then is an example of a structured beginning that sets a specific and immediate direction for the session, based on what is happening with the couple in the therapy. The issue of the couple's conflict dynamic could be dealt with when it arises again during the couples session.

3
Other Important Factors at the Beginning

Connecting

How does the couple feel about their couples therapy? As illustrated in the above case, this may be an important factor for you as the therapist to attend to at the beginning of the session. Couples therapy can be very difficult for partners. Sara and Bethany dread coming to sessions. Roger and Isabella feel an urgency about their future together and are looking to couples therapy to save their relationship. Right from the beginning of the session you may need to attend to how the couple is reacting to the therapy. For example, you might use some humor or some small talk to help a person who dreads the sessions. For the couple with urgency you may need to jump right into the meat of the issue or, conversely, begin at a slow pace to lessen the urgency. The above case study of Clarissa and Walker shows the importance of you as the therapist addressing the couple's reactions to therapy in order to keep them engaged. There are some partners who look forward to couples therapy. It is the one time they are able to talk. It is the one time the partners feel heard by each other. It is particularly challenging to connect with the partners when one likes and one dreads the couples therapy. The issue for you is how to keep a balance with each partner.

Sometimes couples come in and are quite disconnected from the therapy. They may not have been in for a while. They may not have thought about the therapy. They may be avoiding engaging in the therapy.

They may not have a good connection with you, the therapist. As a result, it may be hard to get the session started. They may not remember what you have been working on. They may be apathetic or resistant. It may feel like pulling teeth to get anything going. As the therapist, the couple's lack of engagement may affect you. These are the type of sessions that therapists often dread. It may feel as if you are working harder than the clients.

Thus, one of the most important factors at the beginning of a couples therapy session is connecting to the couple right out of the gate. Many couples therapies emphasize the importance of building an alliance with the couple (Greenan and Tunnell, 2003; Karpel, 1994). This connecting begins with making eye contact with each partner if possible. Eye contact can happen as you greet them or as they sit down and settle in. As you inquire how they are and as the direction is set, it is helpful to look back and forth to each partner. Partners will often notice this and acknowledge you with a smile, a nod or even a stare. This eye contact lets each know that you are there, you are concerned, and you are ready. It also brings the couple into the room.

If one partner starts the session and talks for a while, it is important for you to look at the other partner to check in on how he/she is doing and to let him/her know that you are attending to him/her. Then it is important to have that other partner talk in order to create balance and connection to you. Even if the second partner says, "I agree with Charlie," you need to ask that partner to say more. That second partner needs to know you are connected to his/her concerns as well as to the first partner's concerns. In the case example above it was important that the therapist ask Walker directly if he was OK with the agenda Clarissa laid out.

Part of how the couple may feel about being in couples therapy includes how each person feels about you, the therapist. If, for example, one member is feeling unfairly singled out by you or if one member is feeling less heard by you, this may need to be addressed at the beginning, particularly if evidence of this has occurred in the last session. Sometimes if such issues are not addressed, it may be difficult for the session to be productive and balanced. Sometimes it is appropriate for you to deal with this in a more indirect way during the session. For example, you may make it a point to be particularly supportive of the disgruntled member during the session.

Courtney and Elisa think you are the best. You are saving their marriage. This may seem like heaven—for a while. Then a session may not go well and suddenly they see you as ineffective and unfair. Thus, you need to watch for too much good feeling and too little. In each session you need to gauge how each partner is feeling toward you as the session progresses.

Usual Beginnings

How do sessions with a couple usually start? You need to determine if a usual beginning is, in fact, helpful or whether it needs to be changed. Perhaps the usual way the session begins eats up time without being productive. For example, Mario and Claudette have a difficult time starting each session. They go back and forth, almost arguing about which one of them is going to start. You may need to not let this play out if it bogs down the session. (Or it may be important for you to let them work this out since it may reflect some of their issues.) As another example, Darren starts each couple therapy session pouting. You may decide that this undermines the upcoming session and thus begin the session ignoring Darren's behavior and setting the agenda. As a further example, Melinda typically begins the couples session with accusations of Felix. In this case you may need to have Felix start the session or start the session yourself.

Tone

You may want to set a certain tone at the beginning of the session. Perhaps the last session was particularly intense and you want to create a lighter tone for the session. You may sense that the couple needs some relief from the heaviness of the prior session. You may decide to do some light kidding to start off the session. For example, after a particularly intense session with a couple, you might start the next session with, "I've got my stripes on today." Humor is always tricky and needs to be appropriate for the couple in order that they do not feel made fun of or put down.

External Events

Something important has happened that could affect your couple. It may be necessary for you to check in with them to see if they have been affected by this event. For example, after the Boston marathon bombings, it was very important for some couples to be able to talk about the impact of what had happened. Many couples were affected quite directly. Sometimes it may be difficult to conduct a normal couples therapy session if a couple has been impacted strongly by a trauma. You may need to be ready to let go of expectations and work with what the couple is experiencing right then.

Betta and Daniel arrive for their couples session. It is evident they are not their normal selves as they walk in. They look like they are in shock. You ask them right away what is going on. They describe that a friend of theirs has been gravely injured in a bike accident. It is clear that they are not able to deal with much else, at least until they have talked about the events and their feelings. They spend the first half of the session talking about the event, their friend's condition, and their feelings. You express regret about their friend. You hold their grief so that they may let themselves feel their shock and sorrow. After they have shared their feelings, they are ready to return to their couple issues.

The Red Sox won the World Series! The couple is decked out in Red Sox gear. Positive events such as this can be helpful to mention at the beginning of the session. One partner may have some connection to the team. Other positive events that may be important to process include a promotion, a salary increase, or an achievement by one of the couple's children. Talking about these events is a way of connecting to the couple in an upbeat and more relaxed way than talking about the couple's issues. These conversations can provide some grease for the wheels.

There are also any number of normal external events that can greatly affect a couple's life, raising challenging issues. These include a sale of a house and a move to a new home, a home improvement project, illness in the family, dealing with aging parents and their health, handling holidays, and issues with their children. There may be some specific events which may be important to bring up at the beginning of the session. If the couple has been on vacation, for example, it may be helpful to ask how the vacation went since vacations often impact how the couple is doing in the present.

THE THERAPIST'S EXPERIENCES AT THE BEGINNING

You are searching, scanning, sorting, listening, waiting, and attending. Your mind is whirring, taking in data rapidly. You may feel excited as you begin this journey. You may feel dread, wondering how you are going to get through this session. There are often contradictory experiences happening within you all at the same time. You are active and receptive, thinking and sensing, gathering and eliminating. This requires multitasking, alternating from one process to another. Thus, at the beginning of a couples therapy session it feels as if you are doing many things all at once. This time period requires the ability to hold being uncertain and yet responsible at the same time. You need to sit back and lean forward. The uncertainty can bring up anxiety. As the couple eases into or crashes into the session, you wonder where this can go. You may both like and be uncomfortable with the feeling of being in charge. In this beginning time, you need your own motor revved in order to start. If your motor is not engaged, if you do not have enough gas for the trip, if you are giving off signs of the motor sputtering, you may be in trouble. Somehow you need to overcome your own obstacles and begin the trip. What might some of those obstacles be? Perhaps you are tired of this couple and their dynamic. Perhaps you feel at a loss as to how to handle the couple. Perhaps you have a different idea of where they need to go than they have. Perhaps their issues are too close to home. This is the time (and there will be other times in the session) for you to use your self-knowledge to know what to do in order not to derail the upcoming session.

4
Bad Beginnings

Sometimes a couples session can begin very badly. One person may come in intoxicated, both members of the couple may refuse to talk, one couple member may attack the therapist verbally, one may start on a rant, one may threaten to leave the relationship. You may immediately have your hands full. How you handle the situation could make or break the session or even the therapy. These behaviors can happen at any time during a session. However, they can be particularly difficult, even toxic, if they happen at the beginning of the session. What are you to do? In an extreme situation, it may be impossible to conduct a couples therapy session. In such situations you will need to step in and take control or risk losing the session or even the therapy altogether. One of the therapist's main roles is to provide a safe container for the couple. When the session starts poorly, it is crucial for you to handle the situation in order to reestablish this safe container. You may need to set some boundaries right away. Weeks et al. (2005) discuss the importance of establishing ground rules for couples therapy sessions.

In some sense there is no such thing as a "bad" beginning in that most beginnings can be used to highlight important issues. In the hands of a skilled therapist most beginnings can be directed to become useful for the couples therapy. It is even possible to orchestrate a new beginning by stopping and having a time of silence or actually exiting the room and reentering (either the couple or the therapist). Addison and Thomas (2010) describe a couples session in which Addison, in fact, leaves the room because of the couple's fierce arguing. After a few minutes the couple retrieves Addison and the session starts anew. Couples therapy requires being creative.

Because this section looks at bad beginnings, it would be helpful for contrast and perspective to consider first what is a "good" beginning. Many of the factors discussed above contribute to a good beginning. A good beginning is basically one that starts off the session in such a way that the session will move forward and be productive. It establishes safety for the couple, balance for the partners, and connection with the therapist. A "holding" environment is established in which the couple feels safe to open up and be vulnerable. Not all of this can be firmly established in the first 5 minutes, but it can be begun. An example of a "good" beginning is as follows: the couple comes into the session having talked about what they want to work on in the session. There is then discussion with you, the couples therapist, about this possible topic. You give your input about the topic briefly, tying it into the couple's overall work. Together they decide to move forward with the topic. Thus, you and the couple are in sync and a possible direction has been put forward. In the next period, this direction is explored and laid out. There are still many bridges to cross with many potential roadblocks to come. A good beginning does not guarantee that the session will be productive, helpful, etc.

Now let us look at beginnings that are not going anywhere helpful.

One Member is Intoxicated or High

In one way the situation is simple. Therapy cannot be conducted when somebody is high. However, it may not be obvious that one member is high and/or either member of the couple may deny that one of them (or both) is high. When it is obvious or even questionable that one of the partners is high, you need to address the situation and explain that attempting to do a session would be unproductive. The couple may need some containment especially if one of the partners is quite upset. They may need some direction about how to handle the situation. For example, if the person who is high has driven to the session, you may need to discuss how this person is going to get home.

Both Partners Refuse to Talk

Perhaps the couple has just had an argument. Perhaps they each feel it is useless to talk. Perhaps one is trying to spite the other. There could be many reasons why both will not speak at the start of a session. There are a number of options for you as the therapist at this point. You could try to draw them out. You could address the partner you think is more likely to start to talk. You could speculate out loud about what might be happening in order to engage the couple. You could talk about the feelings that you imagine each person is experiencing. Or in some situations you might tell a couple that you are going to wait until they're ready to begin. This would require that you are willing to sit in silence, trusting that one of the partners will eventually talk.

A softer version of this type of beginning is the non-beginning. The couple is not overtly upset, yet neither is saying much. You may need to employ any of the above strategies to get the session going. Yet there may be a lack of energy in the room or a lack of desire to engage in the work of the session. This type of non-beginning can happen with emotionally disengaged couples, with couples who feel hopeless, or with couples reluctant to open the floodgates. It is important to determine whether the non-beginning is the result of low energy or resistant energy.

One Partner Begins with a Rant

Kelly and Alicia had barely sat down when Alicia, in full volume, began her diatribe at Kelly. You are on alert! The session may be spinning out of control before it has even begun. Right away you need to determine whether this diatribe could possibly be helpful. Perhaps it is the first time that Alicia has truly spoken up and you do not want to cut it off. However, most of the time in this situation you need to step in and slow Alicia down. If you do not, Kelly may be gone because of feeling attacked and unsafe in the session. In reaction to Alicia's rant she may also feel shame and/or guilt.

ONE PARTNER ATTACKS THE THERAPIST VERBALLY

"This therapy is a waste of time. You are not skilled enough to help us."

"You completely took her side last week and I almost did not come back."

Such attacks can be unnerving for you the therapist. You need to get your bearings right away. More often an attack is likely to occur during the session rather than at the beginning. If one does occur right at the start, it is particularly difficult to ignore or delay. The partner is calling the terms of the session and incapacitating you as the therapist. You need to address the situation. Weeks et al. (2005) discuss how, "Clients can easily turn their frustration onto the therapist . . ." (p. 29) and how it is crucial that the therapist addresses the situation. Even if the issue with you is coming from just one partner, you will need to include the other partner to find out where he/she is about the other partner's concern. In some situations you might elect to delay dealing with the attacking partner's issue until later in the session. You might think that getting into the couple's issues will diffuse the partner's upset with you or you might determine that the partners will handle the issue better once the session is underway. If so, then you need to say something like, "I hear your concerns and they are important. I'd like to come back to them as we get into the session if that is OK."

ONE PARTNER THREATENS TO LEAVE THE RELATIONSHIP

Maurice starts the therapy session with a statement that he is not going to put up with Bernice's behavior any longer. He starts to describe the terrible things that she has done this past week. His initial statement implies that he is ready to bolt. He may or may not be ranting. You need to address his not-so-subtle threat right away or it will hang over the entire session. Bernice may hear nothing of what he says because she has been hooked by his threat to leave. Such a threat can easily override any other issue. This effect may well be Maurice's intention.

This type of behavior does not usually happen at the beginning of the session. It is more likely to take place in response to a buildup of tension during discussions as the session progresses. However, as with Maurice, sometimes a partner will lead off with this threat. You need to get the session out of this quandary so that it can be productive.

One (or Both) Begins Way Off Topic

Jaden begins the session with a topic that seems irrelevant and has little or nothing to do with the couple. He is, in fact, wound up and seems insistent on continuing to talk about this topic. You gently attempt to bring him into the room and refocus him on the relationship with his wife. To make matters worse, his wife Belinda joins in with him on this topic. You wonder how you are going to get the couple to focus on doing any couples therapy. You try again to get the couple to focus on their relationship. The couple persists in talking about Jaden's topic. You may then need to be very directive saying something like, "I think it's time to refocus on you as a couple if you are going to benefit from the session." Much depends, of course, on your relationship with the couple and how often this kind of thing has happened before.

Summary of Beginning

You are sitting down ready to start. Where will this go? You are starting the journey. During the Beginning time frame you need to make contact with your couple and start engaging. You have put out feelers and perhaps tested a possible path. As the therapist you are alert for signals as to what is happening. You have walked to the car together and taken your seats. The engine has been started and the car may be rolling down the driveway. Maybe you are out on the road a little ways or maybe you are still at the end of the driveway. Next comes the decision as to where you are going.

Section III
Finding Direction: 5–10 Minutes

5
OVERVIEW

How will you get beyond the Beginning? What will this session be about? If there is a direction put forth in the Beginning, is this the best direction for the session? The Finding Direction period (roughly 10+ minutes) of a couples session is the time that the direction for the session is usually uncovered, laid out, and/or set. It may be the most important choice point for the session because it usually determines where the session will head. The direction can change at any moment, but the initial direction often prevails.

At the Beginning period of the session there may, in fact, be a clear direction. This does not mean that this is the best direction or the direction that will end up lasting through the session. In fact, the Beginning may obscure issues to come. The therapist needs to consider whether the issues, the tone, the rant, the reported events of the week are worth pursuing and developing. Thus, the Beginning period of the session and the Finding Direction period can be continuous periods flowing from one to the other, or distinct and separate periods. For example, a structured beginning with an exercise might reveal a quite different direction for the session to take. Thus, this Finding Direction period is a time to sift through the data you have so far and evaluate where to go.

Being in this Finding Direction period is like being at a huge intersection with many lanes. Sometimes the traffic lights and the lane markers are clear and sometimes the intersection may be chaotic. The couples therapist needs to keep track of all the possibilities of where the cars may go, who goes in what order, who feels entitled, who hangs back, who follows the "rules," and who does what they want, etc. Sitting at that intersection the therapist may wonder whether it is possible to get anywhere productive, given all the issues that are flooding onto the road. Or he/she may wonder if there will just be gridlock and there will be no movement.

When a clear direction can be established early on, the session has a better chance of being helpful. Then there is time to explore different aspects of the issue. There is time to handle emotions that emerge. There is time to work with distractions, resistances, questions, etc. Time! Fifty minutes is such a short period in which to do the work. When a clear direction does not emerge until the session is 30 minutes along, there is limited time left to do these tasks—a much harder challenge. When there is a clear direction, you as the therapist can begin to look ahead and anticipate how this path needs to and can unfold. You can look at the obstacles ahead and consider the tools that you might employ to make the direction work. All of this is happening while you are also paying attention to what is happening in front of you. Your focus is shifting back and forth from what is happening to where this is going to where you want it to go. Your brain is firing on all cylinders.

How does a clear direction get established? When there has been an upheaval during the week, it may be clear that this must be discussed—must, because the issue is too disruptive for one or both members of the couple to focus on anything else. Sometimes a clear direction is established because there is unfinished work from the last session. Also, you as the therapist may decide where the session needs to go and you start with that direction. Often the couple themselves come in with an agenda to discuss. It is, in fact, helpful if they talk before the session about how they want to use the session. Freedman and Combs (2015) describe a session in which the wife comes in with an agenda about her husband. The direction of the session then becomes focused on his career issues, which affect both him and the marriage.

When there is not a clear direction, you are listening, searching, and sorting. Is what Alan is saying now a direction? Should we go back to what Joyce said several minutes ago? What about the theme from last session? What about the drunken bout that Alan had last week that is not being discussed? What about the throw-away hostile comment Joyce made at the end of the last session?

To set a direction you may ask the couple directly, “What would you like to work on today?” This engages the couple to be responsible for the session. It can get the couple talking to each other about what is most important. If the couple differs about the focus of the session, having them negotiate this difference may be an intervention in itself. In fact, this negotiation may become the topic of the session. Often one member of the couple launches into a topic without discussing whether this is really the desired direction for the session. The therapist needs to make sure that both people have had a chance to weigh in on the choice. Even the person who has launched into an issue may not want that to be the focus of the session. If a clear choice is not made, the risk is that part-way through the session when there is not enough time left, an important issue emerges or is brought up. Thus, it is helpful for you as the therapist to get a clear buy-in from each partner for the direction of the session.

6
Issues in Finding Direction

There are many issues to consider when Finding Direction.

1 Are there loose ends from the last session that need to be handled, such as unfinished work, homework etc.? If so, do these loose ends need to be dealt with before taking a new direction? Or will these loose ends themselves lead to a new direction?

2 Do you go with a safe direction or a challenging direction?
If the last session was difficult, it may be important to go in a safe direction during this session in order to provide balance. If the sessions lately have been either safe or stale, it may be time to take up more challenging issues.

3 Is this the most important direction for the couple at this time? Is there something else that is more pressing? Does this direction fit in with the overall direction of the therapy? Are the two partners in agreement about this direction?

4 Has the couple gone in this direction before and if so what happened? Will this session likely be a repeat of the previous sessions? If the couple has taken this direction before, are they ready to go to a new and/or a deeper place now?

5 Does the couple understand the direction of the session? They may be confused.
They may not understand the point of the direction. With a couple from another country/culture it is important for you as the

therapist to know whether the direction is clear and makes sense to the couple. If one partner wants to talk about ending the relationship because the other one had an affair and the person who had the affair comes from a culture in which an affair is not considered something to break up over, then this difference in values needs to be discussed before addressing a possible break-up.

6 Do both partners agree on the direction?
It is important to have buy-in from both partners in order to move forward. If one partner is not on board and/or has a different agenda, that partner may not be fully engaged in the session.
7 Is this a workable direction? Is this direction doable? Will it be too rocky? Is it too far ahead of where the couple is in their relationship right now?
8 Does communication trump all, i.e. will any direction be undermined by poor communication between the partners? Thus, will the session end up being about communication issues rather than about a chosen direction?
9 Is there time to work with this particular direction?
There are about 40 minutes left. Is this enough? If this direction won't take 40 minutes, will there be time to deal with another issue? What if the couple has two issues they want to address?
10 Are you as the therapist prepared to deal with this direction?
Do you have the training for this? Are you in a place today to handle this? Are you ready for what may come up during the session? Are you in over your head?

Sawyer (2004) describes a case in which she sets the direction for a session. She has the husband, Paul, discuss his fears about socializing; something that is very important to Paul's wife Pat. The therapist decides that this direction is appropriate for addressing the gridlock the couple is experiencing. It seems important and doable. As the session unfolds, this direction expands into other issues including Paul's history of friendships growing up, Pat's criticism of Paul when they leave the house to socialize, and Paul's anger at Pat.

Engagement

One of the first important tasks in these 10 minutes is engagement. Are the partners engaging with the issue, with each other, and with you, the therapist? Couples can come into the session tired, leery, anxious, and in all kinds of emotional states. It is so important for you as the therapist to find a connection to each partner and to help the couple connect. It is not enough to establish an agenda. As a direction to the session unfolds, each partner needs to feel that you are on his/her side and are there to help. Even when the couple knows this overall, the connection needs to be reinforced during this Finding Direction period. The developing direction may feel scary and threatening to one or both of the partners. Feeling connected to you allows the work to go forward.

Case Vignette

It becomes apparent during the first 10 minutes of the couples sessions that Derek is pouting. Whereas he is usually animated, today he is sunken down in his chair with a deadpan face. Meanwhile Colleen is overly talkative as if to make up for Derek. You have anticipated some reaction by Derek because you know from Colleen's therapist that Colleen has set a boundary on Derek's constant questioning of her. Is Derek's pouting his punishment of her? How will you engage Derek without unleashing his usual barrage of hostile questions about Colleen's behavior? If Derek remains pouting the whole session, he will undermine Colleen's efforts to set boundaries. You need to find a creative way to engage him without setting off his old behaviors. Inside you are cheering Colleen's efforts to stand up for herself as you have seen how Derek can be bullying in his questions. At the same time you want to keep a connection to Derek. You see his constant questions as reflective of his attachment insecurity with Colleen.

In this example there are a number of ways for you to engage Derek. For instance, you could carefully draw him out by using humor or by talking with him about a different topic that is important to him. The risk is that you could lose Derek and the session would not work. It is touch and go and you can feel the tension in you. Thus, even as you are working on establishing a direction, you must also find a way to connect with each partner.

When there are cultural differences between the therapist and the couple, it is particularly important that the therapist determines whether the developing direction fits the values, needs, and expectations of the couple. When there is not a good fit, the couple is not going to be fully engaged.

Rumblings

Through this Finding Direction period there may be rumblings underneath what is happening. What are these rumblings? The couple may be talking about an issue, but their body language may not fit with what is being discussed. There could be legs vibrating, daggers flying, tears behind the eyeballs, sighs, distracted looks, etc. These are possibly signs of emotions underlying the topic at hand or they may be rumblings of feelings about something completely different that has not surfaced. Rumblings at this stage are common and often helpful. Rumblings may be vital clues as to what needs to be addressed. During this Finding Direction period, it is particularly important to watch for these rumblings because they may signal that the session needs to change direction. There is time to turn the ship and delve into these rumblings. Late in the session the therapist may need to note these rumblings but not bring them to the surface, knowing that there is not time to address them. Throughout the session there can be rumblings. It is an important decision for the therapist as to what to do about the rumblings. Timing is a critical factor in that decision.

When a clear direction for the session has not yet been established, rumblings may be particularly important as signs of what needs to be addressed. They may indicate what the couple cannot raise themselves or even what they are not yet aware of in themselves.

As the therapist, you yourself may experience rumblings. In a recent session during this Finding Direction period you as the couples therapist thought you were going to jump out of your skin. You could tell that the husband in the couple was lying. The husband continued to defend his behavior with unrealistic explanations. His affect was off. His wife had caught him lying any number of times before. What were you to do? You could not be absolutely sure the husband was lying, but you "knew." If you did nothing, the session could go on with the husband possibly lying his way through it. If you confronted him, you risked losing connection with the husband and being aligned with his wife.

This example illustrates the question of whether the rumblings exist in the clients, in the therapist, or both. In addition, should the rumblings be brought to the surface? How clear are they? What do they mean? Is it helpful to bring them out or would it be better to let them either pass or develop further, that is, to see where they go?

Sometimes as the couples therapist you may need to interrupt what is happening and address the rumblings directly. For example, you might say to Brad, "You seem particularly quiet today. How are you feeling?" Or to Bethany, "I can see the steam rising above your head. What is going on?" Sometimes you may decide to make the rumblings the focus of the session. For example, "Janice, for the last few sessions you have teared up when your wife talks about your new house. I am wondering what you are feeling about this move." Thus, there are times to address the rumblings and there are times not to address the rumblings, knowing that to do so will take the session down a rabbit hole into the ground.

Floundering

You sit there wondering where on earth this session is headed. Sometimes sessions flounder during this Finding Direction period. Should you get concerned? You need to trust that something will unfold, that you will come up with a direction, that the couple or you will pull this out in the end. Floundering can happen throughout the session, not just in the Finding Direction period. However, the longer it goes on, the more concerned you (and the couple) can get.

What causes floundering at this stage in the session? The couple may not know how to engage with issues yet. There may be an issue that is crying out to be addressed that the couple is avoiding, is scared of bringing up, doesn't know how to address, is waiting for the other partner to raise. The couple may, in fact, be talking about too many topics at once. They may be interrupting each other and getting nowhere. They may keep changing the subject. These are among the possibilities that are thwarting the session and/or you, the therapist. You need to assess what is going on as you look for possible directions for the session. Sometimes you need to sit back and let the couple play out whatever dynamic is unfolding, before interjecting. In structural therapy this is the enactment stage of therapy (Greenan and Tunnell, 2003) during which the couples therapist watches to see the dynamic between the partners in order to be able collect information to work with. Once the therapist has seen the couple's circular dynamic played out, he/she may then feed back to the couple what he/she sees happening. Often the couple is unaware of the pattern they are creating. In this sense the session is not floundering at all. It is a vital part of what is to come.

Other times the floundering is problematic because it is starting to get out of hand. An important question for you to determine is whether you need to intervene to keep control and to maintain the therapy as a place of safety. The floundering may also be problematic if it is part of a pattern that the couple plays out that makes finding a direction to the session difficult. They may just want to come in to therapy to argue and blame. They may just want to tell stories. They may just be there looking for you to be judge and jury. Thus, it may be important for you to intervene to get the session on a productive track.

The Therapist's Experiences

This is the time when you need to be quick on your feet. In a short period of time you need to synthesize your data and set out a direction for the session. In 10 minutes. Not much time. Yet, you are one-fifth into the session. You need to integrate your assessment of where the couple is today with what you already know about them in order to assess a direction. Even if the couple sets the direction, you need to assess that this direction makes sense, is doable, and is appropriate. This period can feel quite pressured for you, given what you need to accomplish. What if no clear direction is emerging? What if you cannot do your job? This period can challenge your patience and ability to trust in your own skills. You may feel the tension of the need to let things unfold and the need to take charge. Your own style may come into play. If you are a planner and the session has no clear direction, how do you deal with this discomfort? If you are more of a delegator and the couple is looking to you for direction, how do you respond?

This period may also be frustrating when it is difficult for the couple to find a direction. When partners disagree about the direction of the session, it may be a challenge for you to move things along without seeming to take sides.

During this time your job is weighing and balancing, considering and discarding, directing and listening, and looking for the unconsidered. Your head can feel jammed with too much to integrate. You may feel the weight of making judgments about how this or that direction will affect not only the session, but the couple's following week. How will they fare after the session?

Summary of Finding Direction

There you are at the intersection seeing the possible directions to take. What do you do? This time period is crucial to the session as it often sets the direction for the rest of the session. Even if other directions unfold as the session progresses, the initial direction often creates these possibilities. This Finding Direction time frame can be smooth, rocky, clear, foggy, and/or challenging. This section discusses how to set a direction for the session. Now you are, hopefully, ready to plot your trip.

Section IV
Establishing the Work: 10–20 Minutes

7
INTRODUCTION

Ready! Set! Once a direction is chosen, the couple and the therapist need to explore this direction and begin to lay out the work to be done. This is the period of Establishing the Work. It is roughly the period between 10 and 20 minutes of the session. Even though the task of the previous period is Finding Direction, the couples therapist continues to evaluate this direction as it unfolds. There are still many decisions to be made. It is not always possible to cement where the session is going in the Finding Direction period because there can be too many impinging variables that affect how the work unfolds. Thus, although the Finding Direction and the Establishing the Work periods are different, they have similarities given that the direction of the session will be adapted and perhaps changed.

The analogy of taking a trip given in the Introduction is worth repeating. The Finding Direction period is figuring out where you are going. Establishing the Work is pouring over maps, getting suitcases, loading the car, and starting on your way. During this period the direction takes shape and/or can be changed. The next period, Full Steam Ahead, is the actual trip with its detours, stops, change of drivers, arguments, singing in the car, etc. It is the time when the body of the work is done.

It is important to note that some couples sessions go right into doing the work of the session, the Full Steam Ahead period described later. There may be no distinct Beginning and Establishing the Work time frames. This is most likely to happen when an agenda is clear from the outset and it is well connected to the previous session/s. Thus, these distinct periods are not always the way any given couples session actually plays out.

Establishing the Work is the period for laying the groundwork for the direction chosen and figuring out how the work will happen. The couple may be telling the story that illustrates the issues. They may be dancing around their main concerns or they may be caught up in the emotion of the moment. They may be still warming up to engaging with the direction chosen. The therapist is often weighing options, listening for where to focus the work, and waiting for the prime concern to emerge.

With only 50 minutes in which to do the work, why does it take 10, 15, or even 20 minutes to establish the work, even when a direction has been set? Partners may need to be heard regarding other concerns before they can become focused. The therapist may not know where to take the direction yet. There may be strong distractions or repetitious dynamics that are interfering. How does a clear agenda get fully established especially since even when such an agenda is set, it can be disrupted and/or changed at any minute in the session?

In the Beginning section, structured and opened-ended beginnings were discussed. It would seem that if there is a structured beginning, the work of the session is set. Yet, a structured beginning is a trial. It may or may not take. Other directions may emerge. This Establishing the Work period is a time to assess what direction has taken hold and should or should not be pursued. It is common when the therapist or a partner begins with a clear agenda that the focus of the work ends up being a variation of that focus. Freedman and Combs (2002) describe a number of sessions within a case study. In one session they give an account of the direction of the session moving from the couple's sexual relationship to the impact on the couple of growing up female and male in our society.

If the structured beginning is crumbling or if another more important issue or direction is emerging, this is the period to change direction. In this same case study Freedman and Combs (2002) describe another session which begins with a couple talking about the wife's past outside relationships with several men. Part-way into the session the couple decides that they really want to focus on their disconnection with each other as the more important issue.

As the work of the session begins to emerge, you as the therapist must weigh and balance many concerns. What will be the work involved to deal with this issue? Is each partner ready to handle this work? Does it make sense in the scheme of the overall therapy? Does the direction need yet more focus? What are the steps and the timing of the work ahead? What other issues is this direction likely to bring up? Where will this leave the couple at the end of the session? What will be the ramifications of doing this work for the couple during the upcoming week? What is your role likely to be? Are you ready to take this on? What external factors will affect the work and the aftermath of the session? All of this and more are running through your mind at the same time that you are listening to the couple and conducting the session.

8
Setup for the Work

Sometimes the work of a session may take some setup. The setup time may be necessary for the following reasons: to work through resistance, to build concepts needed for the direction, to deal with feelings before the direction is fully set, to deal with other impinging issues first, and to enlist the couple's cooperation and consent. It may be that during this setup time the issues of the setup become the work itself. Since couples therapy can change direction at any time, as the therapist you need to be ready to shift gears if needed.

There are many times when you explain the setup and tell the couple the steps you are taking to get where you want to go. The advantage of telling the couple is that it enlists them in the direction of the work and invites their input. In fact, the couple's input may be vital to the setup working out. The partners may have ideas about how to make the process work or they may have other ideas that take the session into a different and perhaps more helpful direction. They may also raise resistances/obstacles that can be addressed overtly. Involving the partners in the setup is a collaborative approach; one that is used in post-modern couple therapies such as narrative therapy (Freedman and Combs, 2015).

The following example shows a particular type of setup: an undisclosed setup in which the therapist has a direction in mind that is not made clear to the couple. Often couples therapists know what is involved in working through particular issues. Partners may need to be led into the steps as they are ready. In this case, you as the therapist are working to uncover an issue that the couple is attempting to hide.

Case Vignette

Manny and June are quite defensive about Manny's drinking, minimizing its impact on their life. You have heard from their daughter's therapist that Manny had become quite drunk on Saturday night and had fallen down and scraped his face. You can even see the scrapes, but you decide to wait before bringing them up. You pursue a course of setting up the discussion in a way that would make it difficult for Manny to minimize the scrapes. You know if you lead off with bringing up the scrapes, he will pass them off as something else and June will not challenge him. You start with asking them about their weekend, looking for a way to edge up to the event of his fall. You ask them what they did over the weekend. Carefully you watch Manny's face to see whether his eyes harden and his jaw sets. If they do, you stop and look for another direction, still not asking directly about Manny's scrapes.

Another example of an undisclosed setup involves you guiding an unfaithful partner to go beyond defensiveness toward acknowledging that she has hurt her husband. This can be very tricky work, involving finding a way for the unfaithful wife to be able to be vulnerable. The ostensible direction may be helping the husband work through his feelings. The undisclosed direction is your agenda to help the wife shift into remorse. If you were to lead with this agenda, it is likely the wife would, indeed, become more defensive. However, if the wife can see her husband's pain, she may soften and experience her caring for him.

Thus, the undisclosed setup is common in couples therapy. Sometimes, as illustrated, the therapist is intentionally keeping the setup undisclosed and at other times it is not intentional, but just not necessary, to explain the setup. Couples become used to the therapist guiding them in the sessions and expect that they may have steps they are helping the couple to work through.

Elements Involved in the Setup

There are any number of aspects to the setup:

1. Therapist scanning. As the therapist you may need to scan your memory of how well the approach you have in mind works, how well it may work with this couple, whether you have used this approach before, and whether this is an appropriate time to unfold the direction of the session in this way.
2. Treading water. Sometimes you need time to scan and plan. You do not have time because the session is progressing. Sometimes you half-listen as you figure out what to do. Sometimes you let the couple talk on while you are planning. This can be challenging because you may miss something important while you are doing your creative work. You need to be comfortable enough to ask the couple to repeat something you may have missed.
3. Testing the waters. You may need to test out some possibilities and/or approaches before securing the direction. You are putting your toe in the water.
4. Psychoeducation. The couple may need to be educated about the steps to work on together to resolve an issue.
5. Finding a way in. As illustrated in the previous case vignette, you may need to find a way into an important issue or process. As part of this you look for how you need to act, how to manage the couple's interactions, how to help the couple to be receptive, and how best to take the steps forward (step by step, suddenly, quietly, intensely, etc.). This is an art which takes skill, intuition, trust of the couple, and respect for the clients.
6. Positioning the partners. Before a direction can be fully taken you may need to help the partners to be in the best possible place for responding. Positioning may involve any of the following: dealing with certain emotions first, explaining some concepts, getting other issues out of the way, getting one partner to show empathy to the other, or dealing with smaller similar issues before getting to the larger issue.

Freedman and Combs (2015) describe the setup in a session. After the direction of the session is set, the therapist works with the wife to help her to be a better listener to her husband. The therapist does this by talking with the wife about someone in her life who really listens. After the wife identifies an important person and the qualities of the person's listening, the therapist asks the wife to listen as this person listens. Thus, the therapist is finding a way in (as in point 5).

9
The Developing Work
Productive, Trouble, or Unproductive?

When is Work Likely to be Productive?

How do you as the therapist determine if the work developing is potentially helpful? For a direction to be productive given the 50-minute session, it most often needs to meet the following criteria. "Most often" is used as the qualifier here because there are exceptions that will be discussed.

1. The work at hand needs to make sense to the couple.
2. You need a vision of where the work is going.
3. You need to be able to handle what may come up in the session and what may come out of the session.
4. The work needs to be connected to the overall goals of the therapy.
5. The work needs to be consistent with the couple's cultural values.
6. The work needs to address both people in the couple, not just one, even if the focus may be more on one person in this particular session.
7. The work needs to bear fruit before the session is over.
8. The work needs to not leave the couple hanging/in turmoil/arguing at the end of the session. The couple needs to be able to function after the session.
9. The couple needs to be able to leave the session having gained something from the session.

Many couples therapists reading this list will remember numerous times that couples sessions they have led have not met any of these criteria. Couples therapy can be messy because intimate relationships are messy. Couples therapy is not totally predictable. Sometimes as the therapist you do not know where the direction is going. Sometimes you get in over your head. Some sessions seem to go nowhere. Yet, the goal is for the work to be productive and helpful for the couple.

When is the Work Trouble?

Sometimes the developing work is trouble. For example, if the wife of a sex addict feels further traumatized by new revelations of the husband's acting-out behavior, the couples therapy is adding to the lack of safety and trust she needs in order to engage in the therapy. To hear further revelations risks destabilization for her.

Here is a list of types of work that can be trouble:

1. One or both partners become destabilized.
2. The direction of the session jeopardizes the couple's children in some way.
3. The work leads to destructive acting-out behaviors.
4. The work leads to distrust of the therapist by the couple.
5. The therapist becomes overly involved in the issue, losing objectivity.
6. There is not enough time to handle the work adequately.
7. The therapist attempts to delve into work for which he/she is not adequately trained.
8. The work conflicts with the cultural values of the partners.

Most couples therapists have had any number of these experiences. When a couples therapist makes a misjudgment about the unfolding of the direction of a session, he/she needs to know how to pull out of it, salvage the session and help the partners.

Weeks et al. (2005) in their book, *If Only I Had Known: Avoiding Common Mistakes in Couples Therapy*, write about a number of these types of trouble. They discuss lack of adequate training, loss of neutrality, and mistakes of timing that lead to these issues.

As the work of the session takes shape, as the couples therapist you need to determine the possible benefits and risks of the direction. If as the work unfolds, you come to see that there will be problems with staying with the current direction, you may need to think quickly about how to change course, what new direction to take and how to communicate this to the couple. Sometimes you can explain to the couple why the current direction is not working and where you suggest moving to next. The further into the issues and the process the couple gets, the more difficult a change will be.

When is the Work Likely to be Unproductive?

Sometimes a direction may not be trouble, but it appears to the therapist and/or couple to be unproductive. The developing work may not be harmful. It just doesn't help the couple progress. This situation is certainly frustrating for the therapist. It is our job to help the couple. When nothing is coming of the work, we rack our brains for where to go and how to pull the session out.

The unfolding of the work may be unproductive when:

1. The couple is not engaged in the issue or process.
2. There is something more pressing on the partners' minds than the current work.
3. The therapist is pushing an agenda that doesn't meet the couple's needs or desires.
4. The couple is avoiding issues.
5. The couple fears that addressing their issues will lead them to break up.
6. The couple doesn't want to be there.
7. One or both partners are sick or otherwise indisposed.
8. The couple has not done any work between sessions.
9. The couple is stuck.
10. The developing work is a repeated direction from other sessions.
11. The couple has forgotten previous work.

If a direction is unproductive, it may be important to look at why it is so in order to find a better direction. Sometimes any direction will be unproductive. Then it is important to address the situation. Very occasionally a session needs to be stopped. If, for example, someone is not feeling well and is not up for the session, it may be better to end. Most often, however, a change of direction is warranted or a deeper level of work about why the session is not going anywhere is in order.

The Therapist's Experience

So much to juggle! Setting a direction may give a momentary period of clarity, yet there is so much yet to come. There is so much to consider during the Establishing the Work period. Your head can get clogged. Going back to the trip analogy, this is the period during which you are pouring over the maps, figuring out how to carry out your plan. Looking at all the possible routes, traffic patterns, and construction sites can be overwhelming. Yet, this is the time to use your skills to hone the session. It can be not just daunting but exhilarating as you lay down the plans. This period requires both taking charge and watching to see what emerges, seemingly contradictory skills. Left brain, right brain. Your adrenaline is pumping and you are taking deep breaths as you allow things to unfold. Charging ahead and sitting back. Keeping this balance is tricky. Sometimes we do too much charging ahead and have to backtrack. Sometimes we do too much sitting back and the session stalls. No wonder doing couple therapy is so fascinating since it draws on many of our faculties.

Schlanger (2011) describes the therapist's difficult role in problem-solving therapy. (Note that she is writing about doing couples therapy even though she uses the singular word ("client").) This reflects well what couples therapists go through at the Establishing the Work stage of the session.

> The therapist is functioning at many levels at the same time—asking pertinent questions, listening to the client's response, formulating hypotheses, listening to the language used in order to be able to use it, trying to figure out what the client's position is, listening further and incorporating what the client continues to say to modify the initial hypothesis—all in an effort to fine tune and move toward promoting active change, and all this while seeming to not be working too hard.
>
> (p. 138)

Summary of Establishing the Work

This is the time for plotting out the session. You have your direction. Now how will you make it work? You need to create the setup to carry out your plan. You need to make sure the work is going to be productive. You are pouring over the maps, looking at roadblocks, and getting ready to take off. You test out the possibilities, looking at issues of timing and the couple's readiness for the work. In the next time frame you will be on the road. The heart of the work is still to be done.

Section V
Full Steam Ahead: 15–40 Minutes

10
Introduction

Now is the time! This is the meat of the session. This is the time to dig in and do meaningful work. This is the time to roll up your sleeves and commit to the work. For the therapist it is often the most exciting and rewarding time. Something can get done. New outcomes can emerge. This is the period in which something definite happens. The direction has been set, the work has been established and now you and the couple can sink your teeth into the work. In the best of sessions the couple is clear about the work they are doing: looking at the pros and cons of sending their child to a special school, working on how to be more physically intimate, understanding what went wrong in an argument. As the couples therapist, you need to be clear about the type of session you are running. Then you can guide the couple through territory that is likely to be familiar to you. You know options and can envision possible outcomes. All couples therapists have had the experience of not knowing even at this point what the work is about, yet this is not preferred and not the norm for an experienced couples therapist. For the couple this can be the most intense, scary, and unnerving time. The boat has left port and is out in the middle of the ocean. Land is not yet in sight. The couple must trust that you as the therapist know how to keep the engine going and how to steer the ship.

Full Steam Ahead occurs during the time period of 15–40 minutes. Thus, you often have about 25 minutes to really work the issues with the couple. Not much time! It shows how much pressure there can be to accomplish some helpful work during a single session.

However, this 15–40-minute time frame can vary greatly. For example, occasionally a session can jump right into the work and be Full Steam Ahead within minutes. This happens when there is a compelling issue, the couple is fully engaged, and you as the therapist see a clear direction. On the other end of the spectrum, a floundering session may not move into the Full Steam Ahead period until 30 minutes into the session or even not until the end. Part of what makes doing couples therapy so stimulating and at times exasperating is how the unknown can emerge at any point. Many couples therapy sessions, however, go through the stages being outlined: Beginning, Finding Direction, Establishing the Work, and now Full Steam Ahead.

What happens during this Full Steam Ahead period? This Chapter 10 will look at four important aspects of this period of the session: unfolding of the work, disruptions to the work, types of sessions, and roles of the couples therapist. Four categories of types of couples therapy sessions will be covered in Chapters 11–14. Chapter 11 will discuss seven types of Difficult Couples Therapy Sessions. Chapter 12 will present seven types of Classic Couples Therapy Sessions. Chapter 13 will present seven Special Types of Couples Therapy Sessions. Chapter 14 will present five Deeper Couples Therapy Sessions. Chapter 15 will examine how to use intervention exercises as part of the Full Steam Ahead period of the session.

Unfolding of the Work

Once into the body of the session, how do you guide the session so that the work unfolds productively? Much depends on you and your therapeutic approach. There are, however, some truisms that hold in many sessions.

1 You gauge what type of session this is becoming in order to guide it successfully in that direction (see below for types of sessions).
2 You anticipate the steps that are necessary to get from point A to point B.
3 You "listen" for what disruptions might occur in order to be prepared for how they might derail the session.
4 You are alert for how you may get caught in the web of the unfolding session. You look for issues of your own that could get activated

and remember how to deal with them. You anticipate the limits of your abilities and knowledge.

5 You remember prior sessions like this: what may have worked and what may have gone wrong.
6 You look for how to find a new direction if this session becomes a repetition of past sessions.
7 You choose when to show reactions of your own that may facilitate the work. You may at some point decide to show shock, sadness, surprise, etc.
8 You become invested in the piece of work, but are ready to let it go, if need be.
9 You are ready for what may happen. Couples therapy sessions can turn on a dime.
10 You look for what the couple will/can take away from the session.
11 You anticipate what may happen after the session in order to possibly handle it during the session.
12 In other words, you become a wise person capable of handling any twists and turns, any catastrophes, any challenges. You are a rock, a juggler, a supporter, a cop, etc. No pressure! This is a workout of creativity, love, and endurance.

Disruptions to the Work

Resisting

The work of the session is well underway. The couple seems to be making progress. Then one partner doesn't want to talk about the issue any longer. Then one partner becomes evasive or attacking. Then one partner who has been pushing the other partner gets scared and acts strangely. There are many ways in which partners can resist the work and prevent it from becoming productive, and there are many reasons for resisting.

In this section resisting refers to blocking the work in progress. The term "resisting" is used here rather than "resistance" because resisting is an active behavior that is going on right in the room. Resisting may also be a manifestation of a larger resistance in the couples therapy. The larger resistance may need to be addressed at some point, but not now when the work is underway. At this point in the session you look for resisting if it blocks the work from being able to continue.

What can you do when you encounter resisting during the session?

1 Allow the resisting to continue such that (a) it becomes clear that it is there, (b) it plays out and the individual or couple lets it go, (c) it provides material for the work in progress.
2 Observe what is happening and ask about it. For example, "I see that you have become quiet. What is happening?"
3 Ask the partner who seems to be resisting about the underlying feelings. For example, "What are you feeling right now?" Or, "Are you feeling uncomfortable (scared, nervous, vulnerable)?"
4 Come at the issue from a different direction, one that is not as likely to elicit the resisting. Go around the resisting by finding ways for the partner to save face or become more vulnerable.
5 Give support to the resisting partner so that he/she can feel heard and feel more a part of the process.
6 Ask the resisting partner to put aside his/her resisting for now, with your assurance that you will come back to these concerns.

The risk of some of these approaches is that the direction of the session becomes derailed and the resisting becomes the focus. This may be inevitable and it may be better to make it explicit. If this does happen, it would be important for you to acknowledge the change in direction. The hope is that these techniques will allow the work underway to, in fact, continue. If the work does change direction, it is important that at some point you tie the work that had been underway back with the new direction.

Becoming Stuck

In any of the types of sessions presented below, the work can become stuck. Becoming stuck can take various forms: nothing is happening, the couple is repeating issues and viewpoints, the energy for doing the work is low, suggestions by the therapist are not leading anywhere, or the couple stays in blaming mode. The therapist needs to consider whether he/she or the couple will take the responsibility for getting unstuck. When the work becomes stuck, the therapist might reflect this back to the couple and ask them what would help them get unstuck or what they could do to get unstuck. The session then might be diverted into a discussion of "stuckness." This may be an important direction for facing a chronic pattern in the couple's dynamics. This may be the time for the therapist to initiate an intervention to shake things up.

Types of Sessions

What territory are you in? The Rockies, New York City, the desert? A couples therapy session can feel like any of these terrains. One important aspect of this period is that you develop a clear view of what type of session this particular session is becoming or what type of session you want it to become. Knowing what type of session is underway helps to guide you through the work. You can develop a plan and see the steps ahead. You can see the pitfalls and the advantages of the direction of the work. For example, the goal of a crisis session is usually to stabilize the couple. However, the goal of a problem-solving session is to find a solution. The goal of a feelings session may be to break open emotions. The divisions given below are to help identify and clarify what may be the main focus of a session. In each type of session there is a discussion of when that type of session is appropriate. There are also guidelines about handling this type of session, pitfalls that can occur, challenges for the therapist, and the therapist's experience.

And just when you thought you knew what type of session you were in, the session can change into quite a different type of session. When this happens, you need to determine if you think it best (or possible) to go back to the type of session that had been underway or to let the session shift.

A session can be and often is more than one type of session at a time. Thus, even as a couple is developing communication skills, they may also be working on expressing certain feelings. Sometimes two or more types of sessions at a time work together and sometimes they do not. For example, a crisis session in which the goal may be to stabilize and a feelings session in which the goal may be to shake things up would be at odds.

References to case examples of couples therapy are given in any number of the types below. Many published case studies describe the overall case or phases of the therapy without describing specific sessions. These examples are not helpful to this book. Thus, for the case examples used, the authors give descriptions of specific sessions (session 3 or 4, etc.), sometimes with actual dialogue.

Many case studies are written to illustrate a specific overall approach to couples therapy, such as emotionally focused therapy or structural therapy. When a session is described, it is to illustrate some principle or technique from that approach. The goal here is different. Written case sessions are presented to illustrate a type of session, not a particular approach to couples therapy.

Many of the specific sessions in published case studies show the bread-and-butter types of couple sessions; sessions such as Processing sessions and Teaching sessions that are described below. It is considerably harder to find examples of less common sessions, such as Therapist as Cop or even a Celebration session. In addition, many of the published case examples show positive results. It is difficult to find cases that show sessions that do not work. Also, the case examples tend not to show the very difficult sessions, such as Therapist Under Fire and A Session Gone Wrong; two types of sessions that will be described. Thus, therapists get less help with handling these particularly difficult sessions. There are exceptions, such as Addison and Thomas's (2010) case that describes very challenging sessions.

Twenty-six types of sessions are presented here. The 26 different types of sessions are divided into four groups: Difficult Couples Therapy Sessions, Classic Couples Therapy Sessions, Special Types of Couples Therapy Sessions, and Deeper Couples Therapy Sessions. These divisions do not mean that a basic session such as a processing session cannot go deep or become difficult. As discussed and as couples therapists know all too well, any type of session can become mixed with any other type of session. You can be experiencing a quiet teaching session and suddenly be in the middle of a crisis session or an emotive session. The therapist's experiences will be discussed during the specific type of session.

Roles of the Therapist during Different Types of Sessions

Most of the different types of sessions call for you as the therapist to play a variety of roles. Some types call on certain roles more than others. As the session unfolds and you become aware of what type of session it is becoming, you also need to consider what role you need to play during the session. In a crisis session an important role you play is grounding the couple. In a Therapist as Cop session you play a directive role. The importance of the particular role you take in a session cannot be emphasized enough. The role you take may determine the success or lack of success of the session.

To be an effective couples therapist you need to be able to assume a variety of different roles. It is not enough for you to be a supportive reflective therapist or a directive take-charge therapist. Being a couples therapist will require you to stretch your natural style and develop other styles. You also need to be ready to switch roles in a flash as the session unfolds. Suppose you are being the cop because the couple is yelling at each other and paying no attention to you. Then suppose that one of the partners starts shaking and breaks down in tears. Suddenly you need to let go of the cop role and become gentle and supportive. Meanwhile the other partner is still fuming and continues to say angry, mean things. Then you may need to go back to being the cop to create space for the other partner's feelings. Back and forth. In and out. You need to be agile. All the while you are watching for the effect that the role you are taking is having on each partner in case you need to shift again. In most couple sessions the role changes are not so quick or frequent.

Roles that you take in a session involve what you do, what you say, plus the affect and tone with which you do these things. Sometimes you may need to enact a role. This may sound as if you are not being genuine. Yet you do this in response to the situation in front of you. You take on a role because you judge that this is what the situation needs. Even though you may be "acting," you are genuinely responding to what is taking place and to your clients' needs at the moment.

All couples therapists have taken on a role that did not go well. Perhaps you misjudged. Perhaps you got triggered by what was happening.

Perhaps you did not know what to do, so you grabbed the best role that you thought would help. Perhaps the second role or the third role you took was not consistent with the first role you took. Perhaps you stepped in when you needed to back off. You need to be ready for these kinds of missteps to happen and be ready to adjust. Recovering is an important part of your work. You might even say out loud, "Well, I guess that didn't help. Let me try something different."

It can be helpful for you as the therapist to explain what role you are taking and why. For example, you might say to a couple, "I stayed back just now because I wanted to see how the two of you dealt with this situation without me getting involved." Or, "I am being firm with you now because I don't want the session to get out of hand."

In any of the types of sessions that follow, as you take on different roles, you also need to be aware of how these roles affect you and any issues you may bring to the table. Dickson et al. (2011) write about how the couples therapist needs to be "aware of how your own history might impact on your responses to particular situations" (p. 106). There is plenty of opportunity in couples therapy for your own issues and feelings to arise.

As therapists, we are trained helpers. As such we run the risk of helping too much. In a couples session you could do too much of the talking, suggesting, processing, etc. The couple may be passive and/or resistant and/or stuck. As the therapist you may feel helpless, frustrated, stuck, and overly involved. When you see these signs that you are working too hard, you have a number of options: stop, ask the couple what they want to do/where they want to go, process what is happening with the couple, or talk about your experience of working too hard. Anger-Diaz and Anger (2011) write of doing couples therapy, "Don't work harder than our client. Wait for the client to take the lead" (p. 158).

11
Difficult Couples Therapy Sessions

These are the sessions that test you. They test your skills, your mettle, your commitment to your work, and your sense of effectiveness. Why begin with these types of sessions? Because they are the ones least written about. Because they are the ones with which couples therapists most need help. Because if you can get through these, you can get through most types of sessions. Because some readers will focus primarily on this grouping of sessions. In fact, in the case study literature it is hard to find examples of these types of sessions. Yet, these sessions are the most challenging, riveting, and demanding of you and your skills. They stay with you after the session. You lose sleep over them.

All Over the Place Sessions

First you and the couple are talking about one issue. Then you are talking about another issue. And then another issue. You are doing your best to focus the couple, to bring them back to the first or even the third issue, but it is not working. You even tell them they need to focus because there are too many issues on the table. Which one would they like to address? You explain that in order for them to get something out of the session, they need to stick to an issue. Or you even choose which one to address. Nothing. They will not focus. This is probably what their life is like. Or perhaps this couple on other days in other sessions focuses better. What is going on? What do you do?

You may feel like you are chasing the couple around the room or up and down a roller-coaster ride. Sessions such as this are quite frustrating. The couple is not connecting with each other or with you. Why do such sessions happen? The couple may be overwhelmed by their life and their issues. There may be too much that came up that week. Each partner may feel an urgency to address a number of different issues. There may be emotions underlying all these issues and the lack of focus. This type of session is the opposite of Nothing Happening (which follows). There is too much happening. So, what indeed do you do after you have tried in vain to get the couple to focus?

1 You might stop the session and ask the couple to sit quietly for a few minutes while they calm themselves.
2 You might stop them and ask what each of them wants from the session.
3 You could do something to startle the couple in order to break the chaos.
4 You could find some way to shift the feel and tenor of the session thus taking them away from their chaos.
5 You could tell them the session is not working and something different needs to happen.
6 You could stop intervening and let them run on and on until they run out of steam.

These strategies are primarily designed to break the logjam, shift the climate, and find an altogether new direction. What you do depends on what has worked in the past, how much the couple listens to you, how often this behavior happens, how severe the issues are, whether you want to run out of the room or simply yell at the couple. These last possibilities are not real (although they may seem to be at the time), yet taking stock of your own tolerance meter is important in this type of session. You need to know when you could get triggered and what to do when it happens. This type of session tests your patience and sense of effectiveness. You can easily get flooded. As a couples therapist you need to know your best strategies for yourself and the couple in this circumstance.

Case Vignette

Henry and Ayeesha are arguing about the dog. Who was supposed to take him to the vet? Who was going to pay the vet?

Then from the dog they go to money issues. Did Henry make the bank deposit today? No, he didn't because he left his pay check at home. Ayeesha asks how could he possibly forget his pay check?

Then from money issues they go to the groceries. Ayeesha asks how was she supposed to pay for the groceries later on? Henry says they don't need groceries because they have enough food. What do you mean they don't need groceries demands Ayeesha? The refrigerator is empty.

So, what is it that they are talking about? The dog, money, food, Henry's responsibility? When you intervene to get the couple to focus on what the issue is, they ignore you and go back to the same and new topics. You try again by saying what you think is the main issue. They continue with their array of topics. You then ask them to stop, take some big breaths, and stay quiet for a few minutes while their temperatures go down and they can focus. You wonder how on earth you are going to get this couple to deal with any one substantive issue.

Nothing Happening

Then there are the couples sessions in which nothing is happening. Try as you might as the therapist, you cannot get anything going. Often these sessions are accompanied by a lack of connection with the couple. These sessions are among the most frustrating for a couples therapist. You cannot do your job. You worry that you're doing something wrong. You worry that the couple will be upset with the therapy and you. Or perhaps you are annoyed with the couple yourself. Why won't they respond? In a Nothing Happening session the couple may be simply unresponsive and not very verbal or they may be quite involved in a conversation that is going nowhere. Your attempts to engage, ask about their week, bring up a previous topic, ask how they are feeling, or focus their conversation do not go anywhere. Ugh! The time goes so slowly. You ask yourself, "Do we really have a full half-hour left?" These sessions do not usually happen in isolation. Previous sessions may have been slow and unfocused. You may have been doing most of the work. It is also possible that a session like this can follow an intense session. Thus, the reasons for a Nothing Happening session can be varied. The hardest with which to work are the ones that follow previous sessions like them. If a Nothing Happening session follows a session in which something significant has happened, the current session may reflect fatigue or avoidance; issues that can be addressed.

Often in Nothing Happening sessions it seems like there is nowhere to go. What do you do? As you sit there, you rack your brain for ideas. Here are some options:

1. Talk with the couple about the nothing that is happening. Point it out. Describe what you are doing to get something going. Ask them their perceptions of what is going on. Perhaps the couple is unaware that things are stalled. Perhaps they are waiting for you to make something happen. This then becomes a process session (you hope).
2. Ask them how they are feeling about the therapy. If nothing is happening, perhaps the couple is frustrated or thinking of quitting.
3. Talk about the relationship between you and them to see if there are issues there. Perhaps they are not happy with you or something you said.
4. Drop a bomb. Say something provocative. Bring up a charged issue. Uncover something kept hidden. This is a risky strategy; one that you need to know will be helpful and not destructive.
5. Put the responsibility onto the couple (or one of the partners) for making something happen. This involves directly asking them what they want to deal with. It would probably also involve explaining to them how nothing is happening and that they need to take charge of the session.
6. Do something to spark some emotion. Weeks et al. (2005) describe such strategies as supplying the missing feelings and bringing up a topic connected to the couple's situation.

Case Vignette

Melody and Hua are talking about how best to help Melody's elderly father. They carry on oblivious to you, their therapist. You ask them if this is the topic they want to address this session. They do not answer. They become quiet for a few minutes. You suggest they return to an issue they were addressing in the last session. Melody talks about it for a bit. Hua has tuned out. You ask Hua where she is. Hua responds that she is tired. Melody sighs and rolls her eyes. You talk about how it seems hard for them to focus. You wonder out loud what is making it hard. Neither woman responds. You have been through sessions like this with this couple before. You go through your memory files to remember what is effective when this happens with Melody and Hua. You decide to ask Melody to choose what to work on in the session because you see that Melody is more engaged and you suspect that Melody has some issues she wants to address. You pray that Melody will bite. In this Nothing Happening session you try a number of strategies to focus the couple. They do not work. Will your strategy of asking Melody to lead the way work? If it doesn't what do you do next? You feel for Hua and Melody knowing how difficult these sessions can be for them. At the same time you feel the weight of getting something to happen.

Therapist as Cop

The couple is yelling at each other. They pay no attention to you, the therapist. There are sessions in which you need to be the referee, the cop. You might play this role in other types of sessions such as a Crisis Session or a Problem-centered Session. However, in a Therapist as Cop session your role as cop becomes the focal point in the dynamic. The session might fall apart or go nowhere unless you play this role. The partners are arguing loudly and are verbally attacking each other. The couple cannot talk to each other. You become like a mediator in a debate or a referee in a boxing match. You may even attempt to put the focus back on the couple and get out of this role, with little success. It becomes important for you to take the cop role to provide a safe container for the couple.

Max and Cory are staring each other down as they sit in their chairs seething. As soon as one starts talking, the other talks more loudly over the first one. Their communications are heaped with scorn and contempt. They hardly pay any attention to you the therapist using the session to argue their minute points as they volley accusations back and forth.

The session could go on and on like this without strong intervention by you. This is the time to be cop. The goals here are (1) for you to get control of the session, (2) for the partners to calm down, (3) for the partners to see their role in the chaos, and (4) for you to provide a constructive direction for the session. McCarthy (2002) recounts a session with the therapist being cop. He writes:

> As Lauren started her angry cascade, the therapist asked her to take a 10-minute time-out. She left the room and took a walk around the block, with the instruction to soothe herself and refocus on positive requests. Roger was alone with the therapist, who confronted him with his provocative and destructive behavior (p. 645)

These types of sessions can be a nightmare for you as the therapist. Few if any couples therapists want to be the cop. We want to work collaboratively with our couples. This type of session is often very stressful and exhausting. It requires constant vigilance and intervention. The partners often fight the direction you are attempting to provide. Much as the partners need you to take charge, they may ignore you or push back at you, even turning their ire on you.

A different type of "therapist as cop/mediator" session is one in which you as the therapist take over the role of being the person to whom one of the partners is accountable. There are many reasons for why this is not a good idea. It could put you in the position of appearing to side with the other partner. Or, it could make you "the bad guy." So when would this be helpful? In some couples one partner is impeding the progress of the couple's growth by not being accountable. Maybe one is not doing important things he/she says he/she will do. He/she may not be looking into some critical treatment he/she needs. Or his/her lack of movement forward may be related to ADD, addiction, etc. If this partner is in individual therapy, then the role of overseer should most likely be the individual therapist. If the person is in recovery from an addiction, this person may be their sponsor. But, what if these things are not happening? What if the couple is only in couples therapy? Then you may need to take on this role of cop. Perhaps a better word than cop in this situation is coach. How do you take on this role? In such a session you negotiate with the couple how to be in this coach role and you work out the issues it might raise. Then in a further "check-in" session in which the partner has not followed through, you look at the issues this raises and you process what is going on with this partner. You may then continue to help this partner find ways of being accountable. Humor can help in these types of sessions. For example, you might say, "I have my whistle today." One great advantage of you taking on this role is that it often gets the other partner out of this role and thus breaks up a dynamic that has likely become parent/child.

Case Vignette

Carlos and Irina are at each other constantly during the session. Irina is accusing Carlos of not doing what he said he was going to do and of lying about it. Carlos is accusing Irina of exaggerating and only seeing bad things about him. Neither listens to the other. Both are fuming and are loud. You as the therapist stop them regularly, telling them that their dynamic of accusing and defending is not getting anywhere. This does not deter them. You ask them to do reflective listening. They begin this process, but revert back to yelling. You ask them to sit quietly and collect themselves. They cannot do this. So, you go into "cop" mode. You need to talk as loudly as the couple. You need to get their attention and you need to take control. You start with saying "Stop." You continue with, "You two are not listening to each other. You are just yelling and venting. This is getting nowhere. You can argue this way at home. You don't need me here to carry on this way. I want one of you to talk while the other says nothing. If the other starts to talk, I will stop you. When it is your turn to talk, there is to be no accusing. You can only talk about yourself, not the other person. We have practiced this before. I am going to watch you carefully and stop you whenever you stray from my directions. This is the only way anything constructive is going to happen today." Through the session you have to stick to this path, intervening regularly to keep the session productive. In the end the partners appreciate you taking charge. In the end you are exhausted.

Cultural background can play a role in communication style. Two people from a tradition in which fiery exchanges are the norm may not see their interchanges as problematic. They may not appreciate the therapist's "cop" intervention. The therapist may need to talk about the couple's background and work with them to understand the therapy process and to negotiate the therapist's role.

Threading the Needle

Some couples therapy sessions are incredibly tense because there is little room to maneuver. The partners are both upset with each other and are distant. There is a palpable tension in the air that could erupt at any time. Yet, each partner is attempting to hold in the tension because they know letting it out will be unproductive. They feel too hurt, they have little trust that sharing their feelings will help, they have been through discussing their issues before with repeated negative results and/or they are facing an "unsolvable problem" (Gottman, 1999). The partners are each in their corners, often quietly fuming and shut down. Couples often come in the middle of a conflict. Yet, in this type of session the tension is from a specific conflict situation that is part of a pattern. The partners are not going to be helped by conflict resolution strategies. These have been tried. It is likely that one or both of the partners are questioning both whether therapy can help anymore and how they can stay in the relationship. They may or may not be thinking of breaking up, but they are feeling stuck, angry, hurt, and/or hopeless.

This type of session is quite exacting on you the therapist because you must figure out where there is a narrow path to tread. Before such a session you are likely to know what is coming. Hopefully you have given the upcoming session some thought, perhaps consulted with a colleague, and have developed some ideas about where to go. This is not the kind of session to wing it. At the same time, each move during the session must be carefully watched in order to read the subtle and not-so-subtle reactions of the partners in order to determine the next step.

Case Vignette

Janice and Todd come into the office, silent. When you ask how they are doing, they each nod and say tensely, "OK." Clearly they are not OK.

Janice's jaw is set and she is keeping back tears. Todd's eyes are cast down and his face is red. In the last few sessions there has been difficult talk about a woman who had contacted Todd on Facebook. She was an ex-girlfriend from ten years previously, before Janice and Todd were married. Janice knew about her, but was upset that this woman was trying to contact Todd. Todd protested that he had nothing to do with this and had no intentions of interacting with the woman. Yet, over the past five years there have been a number of incidents of Todd's behavior with women that upset Janice. She believed that he was inappropriate with these women and did not act like a married man, often leading these women on. Todd claimed innocence and was angry about and tired of Janice's accusations and suspicions. They have been over and over these issues. Neither can see the issues from the other's viewpoint, although Todd has agreed to be more circumspect toward women.

What can you as the couples therapist do in situations such as this? Whatever you do, it needs to be done very carefully. You could:

1 Acknowledge each of their perceptions and underlying feelings without validating either of their opinions.
2 Help the couple focus on living with their different perceptions of reality, making it clear that neither person is being asked to give up their viewpoint.
3 Focus on the importance of the partners looking at the relationship and what will make it work, given their differences. Focus on their "us."
4 Find behaviors that each can agree to in order to help the situation.
5 Focus on the positive aspects of their relationship after working with the above approaches.
6 Help the couple walk to the brink of their relationship ending in order to appreciate what they have. A discussion about what it would be like to be apart; being clear that you are not recommending this, may help them to come together. This may be risky at this point.
7 Focus on the couple doing things together to reinforce their relationship and get away from the issues.

The most that can be hoped for from such a session is a lessening of the standoff, some softening, and some ideas for proceeding forward. The idea that the partners are going to need to learn to live with their differences is often daunting. If they can begin to embrace this concept, there is some progress. The underlying issue for each is whether the other's viewpoint is too compromising for him/her, portrays him/her in too negative a light to be accepted, or touches on deeper historical issues of betrayal, attachment, and/or abandonment.

This type of session is very demanding on you the therapist. You can easily make the wrong move sending one of the partners into further withdrawal or fury. The fury may come out at the partner or at you. You are often racing through ideas of what step to take next watching the results of each step you take in order to determine whether to change gears or whether to proceed. You often need to support, coax, control, and set limits at all the same time. Even if you have seen the couple in this state before, you may need to find different steps to take than the last time. You are often looking for a way to break the tension whether that is through your own softness, humor, firmness, and/or patience. It helps to remember to breathe deeply.

In the above case of Todd and Janice, you as the couples therapist decide to emphasize that the partners see the situation differently and cannot see the other's point of view. You suggest that there is too much at stake for both of them to be able to give validity to the other's view. You reflect that for Todd his credibility and integrity are at stake and that for Janice her trust in her perceptions and her self-protection are at stake. You then talk about them living with this difference and stopping trying to convince the other that they are the one who is right.

Therapist Under Fire

The couple turns on you. One of the partners says, "You don't understand. You've got it wrong. How could you say that? You're taking sides." These are the nicer versions. Then there is, "You don't know what you're doing!" or, "We're not coming back because you're making our relationship worse." Most couples therapists have had and therefore dread a couples therapy session during which one or both of the partners turn on you. Sometimes you hope that the couple doesn't come back. But then they stay. We have all had those moments during which we think, "They are right. I don't know what I'm doing. I'm not good at this." Often as the couples therapist you are squirming, racing, dealing as quickly as possible with your own feelings so they do not get in the way. You are racing from one approach to another in your mind. "What do I do? How do I get out of this? How do I not get defensive? How do I pull this out before they leave?" Some of the challenges in this type of session include:

1 Where the attack is coming from. Does the attacking partner feel cornered and consequently become flooded? Is the partner masking an issue such as an affair? Is the attack the result of a characterological issue such as narcissism? Does the partner want out of the relationship and is undermining the therapy? Is the partner projecting onto you issues he/she has with the other partner? If the attack is from both partners, has the couple joined together by making you the bad guy? Did you make a misstep and stumble on a landmine? Are you getting caught in a conflict that is between the couple, but is now being directed at you?
2 Did you make a mistake? Did you push one of the couple members too far? Did you forget something really sensitive to the couple? Have you not been holding good enough boundaries? Have you been going in the wrong direction?
3 Is what is happening treading on your own vulnerabilities? Are you getting flooded or feeling helpless? Are you in over your head? Does the issue touch something in your own history? Have the clients picked up on a vulnerability of yours and are they using it against you to avoid issues?
4 Can you save the moment and the therapy? Is what is happening going to jeopardize the therapy work? How do you recover?
5 What is the goal right now? Is it to stabilize, to find insight, to calm things down?

Weeks et al. (2005) write:

> Couples tend to be more combative with each other than with the therapist, but sometimes both will take on the therapist. In some

> cases this may be due to a mistake on the therapist's part; other times the therapist may not have erred at all but rather pushed hard on entrenched system rules that the clients are afraid to change.
> (p. 15)

Depending on the situation, there are various directions you can take in this type of session. These directions depend on: whether this is the first time this has happened, how intense the attack is, how out of control the partner/s has become, how much time you have, how related the attack is to what has been happening, how personal the attack is, and how to attend to both partners' needs. Much as you may feel like hiding, yelling, kicking the couple out of the door, or crying, you must, of course, handle the situation. Here are some possibilities:

1. Calm the situation. If the client(s) is flooded, you may need to try to de-escalate the situation first. This might involve lowering your voice or having everyone take a deep breath.
2. Stop what you are working on and address the partner's (couple's) complaint. Show a desire to understand. Reflect on the partner's (couple's) concern.
3. Own some part of what they are raising, if appropriate. For example, tell them you can see that you pushed too much or missed something important.
4. Explain what you were doing and why.
5. Set boundaries on the attack and redirect it.
6. Go into a supportive mode and reach for their underlying feelings. Look for the underlying fear or pain.
7. Express regret that they are seeing you in this way.
8. Remind them of the positive experiences they have had with you (after acknowledging their upset). Affirm your caring for them and your bond in their work.
9. Pass over the attack and continue with the session.
10. After the session call a colleague for support.

Bagnini (2011) describes a couple's case in which the wife "was in an angry confrontation with the therapist" (p. 72). He goes on to write that the therapist "felt he was losing ground and credibility rapidly and might lose her trust" (p. 72). He decided to address her anger by talking about the issue, the wife's underlying feelings, and the source of those feelings. As a result, the wife breaks down and new material becomes available for discussion.

Case Vignette

Lauren is screaming at her husband Antonio. Minutes ago she was calm. Now she is blaming him for all the problems in the relationship. Antonio looks flustered and at a loss as to what to do. In prior sessions he has described Lauren escalating like this at him at home. He has said that once Lauren gets going, she will rant like this slamming him for a half-hour or more. Lauren has denied acting like this. In the current session you as the couples therapist ask Lauren if she can soften her voice so they can talk about her concerns. Lauren then turns on you, blaming you for not making any difference in Antonio's behavior. "You're not helping. What good is it to come to therapy when you can't do anything useful?" Her face is getting red. Tears are streaming down her face even as she becomes enraged. She continues ranting at her husband and at you. You remind yourself that Lauren grew up in an alcoholic household in which she was often yelled at when her parents were drinking. You then decide to try to reach Lauren through support even though you are shaken by Lauren's rants. You begin giving reflective feedback, saying how frustrated Lauren must feel and how it must seem to her that she cannot get through to Antonio. Lauren rants on as if you have said nothing. Antonio sits silently in shock. Lauren threatens to leave, screaming that you are of no use. You share that you would really like Lauren to stay and that you are very concerned about how upset Lauren is. Speaking softly and carefully, you reach out to Lauren with empathy and caring. Lauren starts sobbing. You give her more words of empathy. As the screaming subsides, you ask Lauren to let her tears come out and praise her for showing the depth of her feelings. The moment of attack is over and you breathe into your own shakiness as you silently let out a deep breath. Any processing of Lauren's behavior is not for this session.

A Crisis Session

Your couple comes into the room not speaking. The husband has discovered that his wife is having an affair. Or perhaps he has learned that she lost her job. It is common in couples therapy that an event has happened that has thrown the couple into crisis: a miscarriage, a child arrested, a holiday family blowup, a job loss, a health crisis. There can be a crisis between the two partners, a crisis that has happened to the couple or to one of the partners, a crisis outside the couple with upsetting effects on the couple, an external crisis not directly related to the couple, a chronic crisis, or a one-time crisis. The most challenging types of crises are those that have happened between the couple. For example, one threatens to break up the relationship, one has betrayed another, or one has abused the other. Boundaries have been violated, emotions are high, accusations and blaming are flying, and threats are bouncing off the walls. When a couple comes into a session in this type of state, the first thing the therapist needs to do is to calm the emotions and provide some boundaries. Sessions such as these can easily get out of control. Partners may yell, insult, threaten, and swear. One person may walk out. As the therapist you need to take charge. You may need to establish or reiterate ground rules, such as an agreement that the couple lets you guide the session and/or no leaving. You may need to interrupt, ask the partners to stop, or tell the couple to take some minutes of quiet in which they can become less flooded. It is often helpful for you to explain what you are doing and why. For example, "I need you to let me guide the session if I am to be of help to you. This means you need to let me interrupt you or stop you. Are you willing to do this?"

One of the challenging aspects of a Crisis session can be getting clear about what has happened. The partners may not be able to describe very well what actually took place. Each may talk over the other. Fragments of the story may emerge in a disconnected way. One partner's version of what has happened and why may be very different than the other's. Each may be vying to convince you of the truth of his/her version of events. You may need to stop and summarize what you have heard so far in order to bring some focus and order. You may need to ask the partners to stop and allow you to ask specific questions in order to get your own picture of what has happened.

The couple is likely to need grounding when they are in a crisis. This grounding may take various forms, such as giving support, establishing resources for handling the crisis, setting some boundaries on the situation, and figuring out next steps. Glass (2002) writes about the importance of stabilization for a couple when an affair has been revealed. To calm the waters it is often helpful for you to empathize with each partner, being clear to reference that person's perspective. You might say, "Given how you are experiencing this situation, I can imagine how scared and hurt you are feeling." In doing so, you need to be clear that you are not agreeing with either point of view.

Sometimes the couple needs to release pent-up emotions, such as sadness and anger. McLendon and Robert Bitter (2011) write about the importance of a couple having "time . . . for processing the pain, anger, grief and guilt" (p. 189) during a crisis. As the therapist you need to find the balance between expressing emotions and grounding in a crisis session.

Another step you might take is to give some perspective. You may put the current situation in the context of previous events and issues for the couple. You might say something like, "Let's back up here for a minute. It seems that tension has been building about this issue for the last few months." You might then remind the couple of work they have already done to handle crises. You might remind them of skills and strengths they have developed for handling difficult issues between them. For example, you could say, "We have worked on situations like this before. Remember how you have worked through such difficulties? Let's review those skills to help you in this situation." The goal here is to set the current crisis in context and to help the couple to cope better.

Some partners freeze or shut down in a crisis. The session may start off with stony silence. You may need to tread carefully not to unleash wrath or add to the freezing. You might observe what is happening and ask, "What would help you to be able to open up right now?" Sometimes it is helpful for you to speak for the shut-down partner/s.

In some Crisis sessions you may need to help the couple come up with a plan to handle the situation. Addison and Thomas (2010) describe a Crisis session in which the couple is arguing and ends up in tears. They write of Addison's, the therapist's, experience in the session, "I felt as if a terrible gulf had opened up in the room" (p. 303). The session ended with a plan that the husband would spend the night at a hotel. This was a way to establish some boundary to their misery and hurtful behaviors.

One member of a couple may be in crisis about what has taken place while the other member is not. Is this a "half-Crisis" session? If one partner is in crisis, the relationship is affected. The partner not in crisis may need to be helped to understand this as he/she attempts to minimize or deny that there is a crisis. Or perhaps the partner not in crisis is trying to steady the partner in crisis. Both partners may need to be helped to understand the appropriate role of the partner not in crisis. Much depends upon whether the crisis is indeed an individual issue or a couple issue. Thus, the issue of what constitutes a crisis may come up in the session. The couple's cultural background may also impact what they see as a crisis. There may even be a difference between how the therapist sees the situation and how the couple sees it.

Break-up

There are some particular types of Crisis sessions that are important to mention because they involve special skills on the part of the couples therapist. The first is a break-up session.

"I'm leaving. The marriage is over!" One partner announces this to the other—in the therapy session! The other partner is shocked, devastated. Even if the relationship has been moving in this direction, the partner hearing this news is usually floored. As the therapist, you too may be shocked. The announcement may take your breath away. What do you do now?

One of the challenges is how to help both partners. They are in very different places. One has been thinking about the break-up and preparing for this moment. The other has likely been hanging onto some hope. Your attention needs first of all to go to the partner hearing the news. What does that partner need? Does he/she need to hear more about why? Does he/she need to express anger? Does he/she want to try to hold on one last time? Then, too, the partner announcing the end of the relationship may need help and support. This may be difficult because the other partner may read your support as supporting the breaking-up.

The session could become quite volatile with accusations being hurled, threats being made from either partner, grief, and/or fury pouring out.

One of your jobs is to keep the session focused and in control, even as strong emotions are coming out. Another of your jobs is to have the couple look at what is going to happen from here, especially when they leave the session. All hell could break loose. You also need to address whether the couple is going to come back. It is best to urge them to do so because there is so much to handle and process.

If the couple has children, you may need to address how the couple is going to deal with the children. It is often best to suggest that they do not tell the children at this point when the couple is in crisis. This is another reason why having them come back is important.

There is an enormous amount to handle in such a session and not enough time to handle it all. This type of session is like driving on a crowded highway with cars going every which way without rules. It can be chaotic and overwhelming for everyone. You have to keep such careful attention to everything that is happening, often changing direction in order to do what you can to help this couple who is falling apart.

Break-ups more commonly occur outside of therapy, before the couple sees you. Although their next session may be in many ways like the above type of session, it is not as shocking because some days have gone by. The initial reaction has happened. Yet, emotions are still high and this session may involve many of the elements described. If the couple has decided together to end the relationship, the tone and chaos may be considerably more manageable.

Secrets

Another type of Crisis session involves the emergence of a secret right in the session or shortly before the session. One partner may admit to an affair. One partner may admit to lying about money. Sometimes the secret is figured out in the session by the other partner. The partner with the secret may not admit to what the partner has figured out. The crisis involves the discovery of betrayal—betrayal that may or may not threaten the relationship. One of the challenges of such a session is that the partners are in very different places. One has known of the secret and the other has not. The one learning of the secret is often deluged with emotions and a reality turned upside down. Another challenge is that holding a secret involves lying and/or covering up. The partner who has been lied to is then dealing with the content of and effects of the secret as well as the discovery of having been lied to. Your tasks as the therapist involve:

1 Deciding how much information to draw out about the secret.
2 Handling the multitude of questions the betrayed partner is firing.
3 Dealing with any external effects the secret has had.
4 Handling the partner's emotions, self-protectiveness, and defensiveness.
5 Dealing with the chaos that the secret introduces as it turns things upside down.
6 Dealing with the expanding distrust of the partner who has been lied to.
7 Looking at what will happen after the session.
8 Helping the couple to get grounded.
9 Setting up guidelines for the healing process.

Swartz Gottman (2004) describes a session in which a couple is dealing with an affair that the wife discovered her husband was having. The session is filled with "contempt, name calling, and sarcasm" (p. 52). The therapist quotes what she explained to the couple:

> A wall has to come between you and Anna (the affair partner) with a window opening between you and Judy. In order to do this, you will have to remove Anna from your life altogether . . . You'll have to hear her (Judy's) rage, her anguish, and her fears about you. This may happen repeatedly, but should diminish if you hear her well. I'll also work to support you both and her through this so no one is destroyed in the process.
>
> (p. 53)

This is an example of the therapist helping the couple to get grounded. In a further session the therapist plays a number of different roles. As an example, at one point she gives support to Judy by saying, "You must feel invisible to him" (p. 56).

You may have a strong reaction to the secret also. You may have developed an investment in this couple. You may be in shock. It may be upsetting to see the turmoil and possible chaos that the secret brings. You may be challenged to remain impartial and balanced while inside you could be boiling. It is likely that the partner who has been covering up his/her secret has also been lying in the therapy. This has undermined the therapy and thus makes it difficult to go forward for a number of reasons. Will the secretive partner continue to cover up or lie? Will the lied-to partner lose faith in the therapy, realizing that the therapy may, in part, have been a sham? Have you too been duped and made ineffective in your work? Thus, the couples therapy as well as the relationship may now be in crisis. In this session these issues about the therapy will not be likely to be a focus. You need to be aware that they could come up, but the immediate impact of the secret will be more likely to be the focus. You may need to sow the seeds of how to keep or rebuild the therapy and your relationship with each partner. Rather than scream at the secretive partner, "How could you?" (which of course you would not do, but might feel like doing), you will need to maintain a connection with both partners and set the stage for the rebuilding that will be necessary in the relationship. At the same time you need to show particular concern and support for the partner devastated by this news. How to do both?

The work involved in handling a secret will go on for some time. This discussion only addresses the first emergence of the secret. Further sessions may involve more Crisis sessions as the ramifications of the secret evolve. More secrets may emerge precipitating new crises.

Case Vignette

During the week Mason has revealed to Yasmin that the family business he runs is in financial trouble—trouble that he has been hiding from Yasmin. The business has accumulated significant debt and one of its major creditors is suing the business. As a result he won't be able to take home any money for some months to come. He has yet to break the news to his two siblings who also work in the business. Mason is the president of the business that he and his siblings had inherited from his father. Yasmin is in shock. She is angry and fearful. She wants to be supportive, but Mason's secretiveness infuriates her. They had an understanding that he would share information about how the business was doing. She thought things were fine.

During the session the couple is all over the place—emotions flying, information bleeding out, accusations, defensiveness. As the couples therapist you decide that the first thing you need to do is to take charge of the session and focus the couple. You feed back to them a list of the issues that are pouring out. You acknowledge Yasmin's fury and feelings of betrayal. Then you focus on Yasmin's main issue: why Mason has not told her the truth. At first Mason is defensive and full of "buts." He says she wouldn't understand all the business complications involved. He was sure some deals were coming through. He thought he could pull it out. And so on. You dig underneath this bluster to Mason's feelings. He resists with more "reasons." Eventually Mason admits that he was embarrassed to tell Yasmin about his business problems. He opens up about the intense pressure on him supporting so many people. He breaks down and says how much he feels like a failure. Yasmin calms down and softens her steely tone. Still angry she also acknowledges how difficult Mason's situation is and how badly he feels.

Next you recognize that the couple needs to decide what to do. The rest of the session is spent developing a plan that includes how they will cover their family finances and how Mason will inform his siblings. At the end you get Mason to agree to give Yasmin a daily update on what is happening. They leave in a still unsteady but not explosive state. The next week will be indeed challenging.

A Session Gone Wrong

The session is blowing up and falling apart. This is much worse than the Nothing is Happening or All Over the Place sessions. This is a disaster. All couples therapists have had sessions that have gone dreadfully wrong. The couple is in worse shape than when they came in. One of the partners threatens to or actually does walk out. One of the partners lies and the therapist knows that he/she is lying. The couple argues and throws threats around. The couple ignores the therapist's input as things get out of control. Weeks et al. (2005) write about the emotionally volatile couple. "These couples engage with each other rapidly and with vigor, and their emotional escalation occurs so quickly that productive treatment becomes extremely difficult. It is akin to a dogfight" (p. 41).

Sessions such as these can undermine the overall couples therapy. You as the couples therapist, are scrambling to try to make something productive happen. Nothing is working. What do you do when the session is becoming a disaster? It is important to have strategies that you can use. Some possibilities are:

1 First and foremost you need to get control of the session.
2 You may need to raise your voice and say, "Stop."
3 You need to get the attention of both partners.
4 You could call it for what it is and say that the session is a disaster.
5 You could set ground rules.
6 You could say that there is going to be a moment of sitting in silence to calm the waters. You could ask the couple simply to be silent or you could ask each person to think about something in particular during the silence in order to help the session. You could then take the session into a very different direction.
7 You could focus on each partner separately, addressing his/her destructive behavior.
8 You could confront one of the partners who may be the prime reason the session is not going well.
9 You could do something dramatic, such as standing up or asking the couple to go out of the room and come back in in a different way in order to start over again.
10 You could remind the couple that they know how to interact in a more productive way and challenge them to use those skills.
11 You could model to the couple how to interact with each other more productively by role-playing a conversation between them, being first one partner and then the other.
12 You could tell the couple what you are experiencing.

Many of these strategies are strategies you may use in other circumstances also. Some are last-ditch efforts to salvage a session. Where Breakthrough sessions can be the holy grail of couples therapy, a Session Gone Wrong can be the train wreck of couples therapy. These are the sessions you dread most. These are the sessions you hope your training and experience will keep you from having. After such a session you may find yourself asking,

"Why did I become a therapist? Was I crazy to take this on?" You will likely be thinking about this session for some days to come, replaying it, and wondering what you could or should have done differently. It is helpful to get support from a colleague to commiserate and, when you are ready, to give you feedback. You will need to have a good plan for the next session. Simon (2015) describes a session which is failing. He decides to tell the couple what he is experiencing and how it might reflect what they are experiencing. "Right now I am feeling utterly worthless—not just as a therapist, but as a person—and I am pretty sure that that this is the way that the two of you feel deep down, most of the time" (p. 381). In fact, this stuns the couple and gets them to engage with each other productively.

12
Classic Couples Therapy Sessions

Now to the basic bread-and-butter types of couples therapy sessions. Why present these types of sessions when they incorporate basic skills all couples therapists should know? The goal here is not to discuss specific processing skills or teaching skills. Rather, it is to look at what a whole session that focuses on processing, or teaching, or problem-solving involves. Using processing skills somewhere in a session is not the same as a session that is primarily devoted to processing. Using problem-solving skills somewhere in a session is not the same as a session primarily devoted to problem-solving. What is fascinating here is to understand what is involved in a particular type of session. Understanding the dynamics of handling the type of session you are in is crucial to being an effective couples therapist. You can then better guide your couple through the session.

Processing Couples Dynamics Session

This is the meat of couples therapy. Almost all approaches to couples therapy deal with the dynamics between the partners. How can you not when the dynamics are vibrating in the room right in front of you? For example, Danielle berates Allison for not taking out the garbage, for not being stern enough with their son, for not being sexual enough with her. Allison responds by taking the blame and explaining how she is deficient because of her mother's coldness and neglect during her childhood. Danielle begins to feel badly for Allison and stops the berating. It works! Yet, does it? Allison ends up feeling worse about herself and Danielle doesn't get a fully participating partner. In a processing session the therapist would explain the dynamic that is being played out. This dynamic is sometimes called the persecutor–victim dynamic. There are other classic dynamics such as the pursuer–distancer dynamic, dominant/dependent, etc. When the dynamic is happening in the room, the immediate feedback can be particularly helpful because the therapist can help the couple to see what is happening. Processing sessions can also be about interactions that took place outside the session. Together the couple and the therapist review the couple's earlier interactions looking for the dynamics that took place.

Apfelbaum (1995) describes a fascinating case in which he unravels the dynamics of a couple around their sexual relationship. Here is a sample from a session.

> I (the therapist) also said that Jack and Jane were caught in a familiar circularity: Jack felt rejected by Jane's apprehensiveness and then had to bypass her in order to get turned on. Jane felt somewhat relieved by Jack's autonomous style but felt sexually inadequate with him. This made her feel cold, as did Jack's jibes about her body and his "begging." The colder she felt, the more Jack had to turn *himself* on, using her only as a prop.
>
> (p. 30)

These Processing sessions can be among the most exciting sessions because they get at the heart of the couple interactions. Seeing the dynamics can create real ahas for the couple. The partners can be amazed to see what is taking place. Beyond pointing out the dynamics, you as the therapist may then include instructions that can change the interactions. For example, you may say. "I'd like you to try turning to your partner and saying the following . . ." When this happens, the whole dynamic can be changed right there in the room. How amazing!

When is a Processing session helpful?

1 When there are clear couple dynamics happening in the room, particularly when these dynamics are creating conflict and impasse in the relationship.

2 When there has been a difficult and/or unnerving incident between the partners during the week.
3 When the couple is stuck in resolving the content of an issue because of their interactions.
4 When unraveling the couple's dynamics would free the couple to become closer and more of a team.
5 Often and regularly.

Processing sessions can change the couple's dynamics, freeing them from chronic frustration and allowing them to function more effectively. Processing sessions can be immensely satisfying because the results can be immediate. However, long-term dynamics need to be addressed over and over. Ingrained couples' patterns are hard to break and rewire.

Fishbane (2010) describes a couple session in which she uses the "vulnerability cycle diagram" (p. 223) to help the couple discover "the dance of Lisa's criticism and Eric's defensiveness, justification and withdrawal" (p. 223). Each partner fills in his/her part of the diagram resulting in the recognition of their circular dynamic. Strategic and structural therapies (Keim and Lappin, 2002) focus on surfacing and then altering this circular dynamic in couples.

Processing sessions can be quite exacting for you as the therapist. You need to pay very close attention to what is said and how it is said so that you can repeat it back to the partners. You need to have the precise wording, the tone, and the body language that accompanied what was said. During the feedback you need to be able to say, for example, "Janine you said to Margaret, 'You don't know what you're talking about.' When you said that you leaned forward and your face got red. Margaret you then sank into the chair, starting crying and said, 'What's the use?'" Beyond this feedback you then need to explain the effect of both women's behavior and how it plays into their dynamic.

Thus, you need to carefully observe, remember, and plan how to capture the moment through giving effective feedback that the partners can hear and not receive as judgment. It is easy for either partner to interpret the feedback as you taking sides against him/her. It is often helpful to check in with the partners about how they are receiving the feedback you are giving.

Processing the Last Session

The last session was quite something! Perhaps it was intense, or revealing, or frustrating, or a breakthrough. When the last couples session has been particularly intense and/or difficult, it is important to take the time to process what happened, how each person reacted, and what has developed since.

One week Joshua and Colleen start their couples session by saying that the last session had been the hardest session they had had to date. This is a clear signal that the current session needs to be a session for processing what happened in that last session. The couple needs to talk about what was so difficult and how they reacted. Part of what emerges in the current session is some misunderstanding of what you the therapist had said and meant during the last session. Joshua had felt that you had accused him of being a liar. You need to go over how Joshua had heard this, what he felt, and what, in fact, you meant by what you said. This can be delicate, requiring you to balance your memory of what you said against Joshua's feelings. Fortunately, this couple tells you of their reactions. More often you have to figure out for yourself that the couple needs this type of a Processing session.

There are often indicators as to when processing the last session is needed. For example:

1 When the last session has been very emotional or conflictual.
2 When the last session has been confusing and there is a need to do some sorting out.
3 When the last session included an experiential exercise introduced by the therapist.
4 When the last session was a Crisis or Breakthrough session.
5 When, as in the above example, one or both partners have an issue with the therapist stemming from the last session.
6 When some important and new information emerged during the last session.
7 When a major decision was made in the last session. It is important to check back in with the couple about changes or developments since.

Processing helps to clarify, teach, calm, direct, clear misunderstandings, and stabilize. If the processing is not done and the next session moves into another area, the couple may not be able to be open to and absorb the new direction. There may be tensions that are not addressed. Old cycles may be perpetuated. This processing may take only a part of the next session or the whole session. As the therapist you need to be alert for how well the couple has integrated the last session. They may be still deeply immersed in it and need time to unravel what happened and how they felt. You may need to calm them and help them to do some sorting out in order for them to learn and to move on together. Or they may have pushed the session out of awareness and gone on as if nothing happened. One of the frustrating experiences for you may be hearing that a significant session has been ignored and pushed out of consciousness. You may need to spend some time in this next session shaking the couple up a bit, focusing them on the importance of what took place in the last session. This may feel like trying to move a boulder. Two of the challenges of this type of session are not repeating the last session and helping the couple to see that the current session is helping them to gain something.

Sometimes processing the last session helps to further develop new learnings from the previous session. Freedman and Combs (2002) describe a case study in which the therapist used a reflecting team during a session. The learnings from this experience provided a powerful turning point in the therapy. During the subsequent session the therapist drew out these new learnings to help the couple solidify their newly developing ways of seeing each other.

Teaching Session

Some couples therapy sessions are predominantly Teaching sessions. For example, you might be teaching a couple how to live with differences between them. Part of this teaching might include explaining various approaches to them, such as: learning to understand each other's point of view, finding strategies to handle their differences, exploring the issues that underlie the differences, learning how to take care of certain needs on their own, and turning to other appropriate people to meet their needs. Hamburg (2010) describes a session in which she teaches a couple about boundaries. She writes about how in the early phases of couple therapy "there is a good deal of direct teaching on my part in the session" (p. 318).

These concepts may take a fair amount of explaining, consuming a good part of the session. It is important when teaching to take time to apply the teachings to the couple's issues during that session. The teachings need to be made real for the couple. Concepts are useful when the couple can apply them to their issues right away. In the above example, you might ask them which of these approaches they think would be most helpful to them and then begin to work on that approach, right in the session.

But, you may think, teaching focuses too much on you as the authority. As a therapist you are supposed to be a process person, not a teacher! Yet, couples usually come to couples therapy because of the lack of knowledge about how to address issues. Concepts such as "I" statements may be foreign to them. In fact, some couples ask outright for information saying things like, "How do we do this," or "How does such and such work." Even in narrative therapy, a post-modern approach which emphasizes a collaborative non-authoritative approach, the therapist may work with the couple both teaching and drawing out concepts from the couple. Freedman and Combs (2002) give an example of this in a case study. The therapist draws out the wife about her negative body image and offers the wife some teaching. The authors write of the therapist who was describing a conversation with a model to the wife:

> I told her (the wife) the model had said that people in ads were a very small percentage of real people who were being photographed at a particular age that would not last. These people had been freshly made up and positioned in a particular way to create a particular impression. Furthermore, the final image was often airbrushed to "improve" it even more.
>
> (pp. 331–332)

Frequently, teaching happens in small chunks as a couple interacts. This type of teaching would likely fall into the next type of session, a Skills Development session. Yet, there may be times when it is important to address an overall concept in one session. In order to progress, you may need to explain a complex idea and its application. Sometimes the teaching may be more content-oriented than process-oriented. For example, if a couple is considering adoption and you are knowledgeable about the adoption process, you may take some time to explain this process to them. When teaching specific content, you need to be sure that the information you are passing on is current and accurate. It is important for you to know when you do not have the information that the couple needs. It can be tempting to give them incomplete information that is not helpful.

Another type of Teaching session may be passing on and discussing resources for the couple. For example, a couple may be struggling with resources for elderly parents. In addition to teaching the couple the options available, you may need to help them evaluate those resources.

Another type of Teaching session involves modeling. In a modeling session you as the therapist demonstrate the behaviors you want the couple to learn. This can happen in a number of ways. You could role-play a conversation between the couple with you playing each part. In this role-play you show the back and forth between the partners illustrating how they could have a constructive conversation. Then you might discuss what you did and/or have the couple practice their own version of the conversation while you coach them. Another type of modeling session is one in which you interact with just one of the partners, showing both members how to "handle" dealing with this partner and/or the issue at hand. The partner watching sees an alternative way of interacting—alternative to what he/she usually does. It is critical to the effectiveness of these processes that you discuss what you did and how the couple reacts to your modeling. Did it seem helpful, realistic for them, doable, etc.? Modeling may be the centerpiece of the session or it may be only one part of a session. It can be a very effective way for couples to learn because they get to see an interaction "live." Often couples are grateful to see what you are describing actually illustrated.

There are times when a modeling session is not helpful. This includes: when modeling would elicit feelings of inadequacy in one or both of the partners; when modeling would create an imbalance in the couple (the watching partner feels left out or the interacting partner feels picked on); and when modeling creates too high a standard for the couple.

Thus, a Teaching session is appropriate when:

1 In order for the couple to progress, they need some important knowledge.

2. The couple is faced with a particular dilemma that requires information that you as the therapist can share in a helpful way.
3. The couple is looking for and/or is receptive to acquiring some new knowledge.

There are times when a Teaching session seems indicated, but, in fact, it is not. Sometimes couples seem to need a Teaching session when, actually, there are emotional issues that underlie the discussion. You need to be ready to transition into dealing with these emotional issues rather than continuing to teach even if it means stopping in the middle of giving the information. Other contraindicators include: the couple is not ready for the information, the couple is saturated and cannot absorb the information, the information would be too disruptive to one or both of the partners, or the couple is looking too much to you as the authority. As the therapist you also need to watch for getting carried away with the importance and/or the fun of doing the teaching. Your couple may have tuned you out as you run on too long.

A Skills Development Session

How do couples move forward through their issues? Skills Development sessions are a fundamental of couples therapy. That is, they give the basics of relating. Some sessions are devoted to building specific skills such as listening, problem-solving, giving feedback, time management, parenting, financial management, and sexual skills. Thus, the skills may be either in a specific content area of life or may be more process skills such as communication. In a Skills Development session the couple learn skills and apply them in the session. What makes this type of session different than a Teaching session is that it is focused on the application of skills. What makes this type of session different than a Processing session is the focus on specific skills rather than on the dynamics of the relationship. Clearly there is considerable overlap in these three types of sessions. For example, a predominantly Skills Development session usually involves some teaching and processing. What makes these three types of sessions distinct involves where the emphasis lies, which also affects how the session unfolds. Because these three types of sessions overlap, it is important that the therapist has a clear idea which type of session he/she is conducting. Otherwise the focus may be blurred and something, the teaching, the processing, or the skills development, may get short-changed. Even if the therapist moves back and forth between these three areas in a session, it is most helpful that one of the areas be the primary focus.

Most forms of couples therapy include building skills. The more behavioral forms, such as cognitive behavioral therapy and strategic/structural couples therapies, particularly focus on specific skills that couples can use often right there in the session (Baucom et al., 2015; Keim and Lappin, 2002). Baucom et al. (2015) describe a case in which the therapist incorporates speaker–listener skills, decision-making skills and anxiety management skills. Epstein and Baucom (2002) write of the importance of skills building, "empirical findings indicate that . . . behavioral interventions involving skills-building techniques have produced significant increases in relationship adjustment" (p. 218).

Some skills are necessary for doing couples therapy at all. Thus, if a couple is arguing and blaming each other frequently, it may be impossible to work on such issues as sexuality and parenting. Communication skills usually supersede all else in couples therapy. Since few people are taught how to communicate well in an intimate relationship, much of couples therapy is spent working on these skills. The challenge of this type of Skills Development session is keeping the couple focused on the communication aspect of the work, not just on the issue.

Some couples seek out a couples therapist who has a specific skill set, for example, a sex therapist, an addiction therapist, or a couples therapist trained in disabilities, LGBTQ issues, multicultural issues, etc. As specialists such as these work with a couple, they will describe the relevant skills, have the couple apply them in the session (as appropriate), and/or give them as homework for the couple. For example, the therapist may have a couple facing medical issues fill out an illness genogram to help them, "better understand the family's general scripts about illness" (Ruddy and McDaniel, 2002, p. 710). A couples sex therapist might give a couple skills-based homework, such as Master and Johnson's sensate focus. Apfelbaum (1995) presents a such sex therapy case with appropriate homework.

Thus a Skills Development session is appropriate when:

1 The couple is stuck in a negative circular communication pattern.
2 The couple needs communication skills in order to be able to adequately address any issues.
3 The couple needs content skills to move forward on a particular issue.

One of the challenges of a Skills Development session involves the partners' ability to absorb and make use of the skills. Do they understand the skills being presented? Do they see how to use them? Sometimes by having the partners practice the skills right there in the session, you as the therapist can guide, assess, and give feedback to them as they stumble their way through the skills. Another challenge of a Skills Development session is focusing on an appropriate chunk of the skills that can be absorbed by the couple in the current session. They need to leave with something they feel is worthwhile and usable or they may feel that they have wasted their time. It is important not to overwhelm the couple with too many chunks of skills at once.

As the therapist, Skills Development sessions can feel like you are talking to the wall when one or both partners look at you blankly or barrel along as if you have said nothing. Often you are introducing ways of interacting that are foreign to the couple. They may not see the point of using these skills. Learning new skills means going through an uncomfortable and awkward period of learning and practicing—like most forms of new learning. Skills Development sessions can be frustrating and/or tedious for the couple and the therapist. They can also be quite exciting and empowering to the couple as they see ways out of their dilemmas. Often when partners utilize the skills right there in the room, the interaction between them can change markedly. It can be wonderful to see how one or both partners open up and a new energy is created in the relationship. A Skills Development session can be one of the most gratifying types of sessions because changing an interaction pattern right there can break through how a couple feels toward each other right in the room. They can go from a stuck and perhaps hopeless or angry place to a close and appreciative place within the 50 minutes.

Each couples therapy approach has a specific set of skills to teach a couple. Although different schools of thought may disagree on what skills are crucial for couple development, there is more agreement than disagreement. For example, most approaches address blaming and accusing as negative interaction patterns in couples. As an example, most couples therapists are familiar with John Gottman's Four Horsemen of the Apocalypse (1999). From his research on couples, Gottman has identified these four frequent and challenging styles of interaction: stonewalling, defensiveness, criticism, and contempt.

Case Vignette

Paul often dominates the couples therapy sessions. His monologues are dotted with criticisms of Frank. Frank usually agrees with him adding how he is inadequate because of how he grew up. As the therapist you decide to have Frank work on self-expression skills and Paul work on holding back. First you ask Paul to back off and say less while you focus on drawing Frank out more. In addition, you tell Frank that he is not to say negative things about himself. As he begins to talk, you hear Frank's anger at Paul. You then encourage Frank to voice his anger while Paul listens. You guide Frank through halting attempts to speak up, giving him support and specific skills to express his anger. The result is that Frank begins to find his voice and Paul, although struggling with Frank's anger, is relieved to feel him being more present in the relationship. Paul visibly softens as Frank grows stronger. As the two of them become more connected, you reinforce the skills for sharing their angry feelings in a constructive way.

A Diversion Skills Development Session

How about a couple learning skills that they do not know they are learning? Most Skills Development sessions focus directly on the skills on which the couple is working. However, there is a type of skills session in which the therapist leads the couple in an unrelated direction in which the skills being learned are not apparent. For example, Ronald and Janelle are talking about how they don't communicate very well about their inner thoughts and feelings about each other. Ronald gets off track and starts talking about his father. As he does so, he begins to feel some emotions. You decide to pursue this apparent tangent, seeing an opportunity for Ronald to share some deeper feelings. The more Ronald talks about his father, the more emotional he becomes. Tears flow out from a deeply hurt place. Janelle does not know how to respond to him. You guide her to be able to be supportive. The experience brings Ronald and Janelle closer. In the last 10 minutes of the session you talk about the sharing they have done and the skills that they have used to get closer. You compliment them on their work and discuss how they might be able to carry this work over to their relationship directly. This example shows how sometimes couples can find skills that they need for their relationship in topics that seem like a diversion. This couple finds some skills they did not know they had and did not know they were using. Sometimes this indirect approach can work even better than a more direct approach which can bring up self-consciousness and defensiveness.

A Problem-centered Session

Dana wants Clark to agree that they won't stay at his sister's house over Christmas. Erlene and Janice are in debt and their finances are in disarray. Michele has MS which has resulted in a lack of a sexual life with her husband Ted. What do they do? These couples come in with specific issues to discuss. The issue may be related to something that has happened during the week. However, there is a larger issue that needs to be resolved. The couple needs a direction. They need some steps to take in order to work out the larger issue. Thus a Problem-centered session is one in which the focus is a particular issue. The goal is to make some progress in the session in order for the couple to (1) feel better, (2) communicate better, and (3) figure out what to do. The work in this type of Problem-centered session will often consist of developing steps as part of an overall plan.

Problem-centered sessions are indicated when:

1 The couple is in trouble over an issue right there in the session.
2 The couple has had a specific problem arise that is a manifestation of a larger issue.

3 The couple needs help developing some strategies.
4 There is an issue with immediate ramifications and consequences.
5 There is an issue that requires immediate steps to be taken.

There are a number of challenges in Problem-centered sessions. One of the main challenges is keeping the session on track. Couples tend to get into telling the story of the issue. They can go on and on, making it hard for the therapist to find a way in. They can easily get into "he-said-she-said" debates. The session can feel like a food fight. As the couples therapist you need to be able to interrupt and to direct the discussion. On the one hand, you need to find out enough information about the issue and hear each partner's perspective. On the other hand, the session can easily be consumed by the partners' often passionate accounts. Commonly couples will interrupt each other during such interactions. They will talk over each other, not even listening to one another.

Sometimes the opposite will happen: you will have difficulty getting enough information and enough of the story to work with the issue. This challenges your ability to draw the partners out—to find the right questions and the right focus on the issue to open the door.

Another challenge in a Problem-centered session is figuring out which problem is the most important one to address now. For example, Brad is accusing Henry of making a mess of their vacation. Suddenly Henry veers off into a completely different, seemingly unrelated topic. The new topic, how Brad forgot to submit the taxes this week, ramps up the emotions of both partners. Often couples get too many issues on the table at once. When this happens, there are a number of challenges for you as the therapist. Is the new topic relevant or not? Is it perhaps more important than the topic at hand? Does it shed light on the topic at hand? Do you as the therapist allow the new topic to be discussed because the partner bringing it up often does not speak up? Is the new topic a retaliation, a distraction, a defense? Thus, you must evaluate what the new topic is about and what to do with it.

Most often when a couple gets too many topics on the table, you need to refocus the session on the direction of the work that is already underway. There is likely not enough time to go into this new topic. New couples therapists may have trouble keeping the session focused. Even experienced couples therapists may have trouble herding the couple when they are in high conflict or avoidance.

Another challenge during a Problem-centered session is process skills. Does the couple have the communication skills or problem-solving skills to work on the issue? If not, the session may need to become a Skills Development session. There may be a tension between process and content, that is, to what extent can the session focus on the issue versus the process of communication or problem-solving? The couple usually wants to leave the session with some direction, if not answers, about the content of the problem. If they do not have the skills to get there, part of your work is to balance the necessity of focusing on skills building and finding the road to problem-solving the issue.

Certain issues have protocols for addressing the problems. For example, when a partner has had an affair, one of the first steps is to address contact between that partner and the affair partner. When contact with the affair partner continues, healing between the partners becomes difficult if not impossible. Scharff and Bagnini (2002) write, "Spouses cannot work on their relationship while one of them has another intimate partner at the same time" (p. 80). If a particular couple is not having sex, one of the first steps is to find out if there are any physical issues that impede sexuality, such as medications or hormonal issues. Thus, information needs to be gathered, boundaries of behaviors may need to be established, steps of healing may need to be explained, guidelines within the therapy session may need to be established, and the role of the therapist may need to be explained. A realistic assessment of the issue needs to be developed and explained to the couple. Expectations of what can happen in therapy and in this particular session need to be established. Couples want the problem solved now. One of the pitfalls of Problem-centered sessions is that the problem in all its painful ramifications gets laid out and then the session is over. The couple is left open on the operating table. Thus, you must balance having a period of exploration of the problem, a period of working on the issues, and a time of closing, in order that the couple can leave the room somewhat intact. Therapy needs to be a safe container.

It can be easy for the couple and you as the therapist to get overwhelmed during a Problem-centered session. The problem may seem insurmountable. It may seem all-encompassing. It may seem intractable.

It is your job to break off chewable parts of the problem and to decipher and explain some aspect of the issue that can be realistically addressed in the current 50-minute session. Thus, the result of a session dealing with an affair may be that the partner who was having the affair agrees not to go to a particular work conference where he/she would see the affair partner. Or the couple dealing with one of the partners' difficult family members agrees that they will stay at a hotel when they visit the family and not at the family's home. Couples need to see that something can be done. They also need to be shown that the problems are often resolved in small steps.

Another challenge of a Problem-centered session is your knowledge about the issue. Do you have experience working with this issue? If you do not, you may need to delay addressing the issue until you can run home and read about the issue or call a colleague. Sometimes you may need to learn about the issue from the couple if it is appropriate. For example, a couple may need to explain the steps they are going through to address infertility. Or one of the partners may need to explain the cultural dynamics of his/her family and how this impacts the couple. Thus, you need to assess how much you need to know about the issue and from where to get this knowledge. You may even need to refer the couple to someone with particular expertise about this issue.

Since most couples come into therapy with more than one issue, they may focus on one issue one week and a different issue the next week. This presents a particular challenge for a Problem-centered session because the current issue may not get readdressed right away. Since no issue is going to get resolved in one session, how do you guide a meaningful session which opens up the issue and provides closure at the same time? Running such a session is like having a zoom lens that is being adjusted throughout the session. Sometimes the lens is up close and focused on one aspect of the issue. At other times the lens pulls back and looks at the larger picture. You need to watch and guide the lens adjustment such that something meaningful gets accomplished and is tied into the couple's larger issues. This dance takes your constant attention and decision-making.

Problem-centered sessions can be particularly difficult because they often address deeply held beliefs, standards, and expectations that each partner has developed over his/her life. Dickson et al. (2011) describe a

Problem-centered session in which the core beliefs, standards, and expectations held by the couple are uncovered.

This work can be like slogging through the trenches. In addition, couples dynamics may have developed that further bind the partners to their viewpoints. This may have developed because the partners feel threatened by the other's views and behaviors, because they cannot undertand the other's views, because their sense of self is wedded to their own view, because they feel betrayed, etc. In the session you need to determine what is causing the tension and disagreement. Some Problem-centered sessions are focused on rooting out these deeply held views. Getting them out in the open can often help the couple to see beneath the immediacy of the issue. Sometimes seeing such underlying views may make resoltion harder because one or the other partner may be discouraged or upset or by what he/she sees.

Part of your work is to help the couple find possible directions for addressing the issue. When the couple finds ideas and possible solutions themselves, they are more likely to implement them. You need to resist coming in too quickly with your own directions for the issue. When you do come in with your own ideas, it is helpful to put it to them as a suggestion and follow-up by asking the couple what they think of the idea. Goldman and Greenberg (2010) give a case with actual dialogue from individual sessions. In one of the sessions the therapist, Goldman, is addressing the wife's cutting behavior. She says to the wife "... I am wondering if you could, instead of having to hold on to all of it (her bad feelings), could you just come to Jeff and say, 'I am feeling pretty bad right now and I am thinking of hurting myself'" (p. 265). She is suggesting an action for the wife to take. It can also be helpful to suggest a number of different ideas so the couple can consider their own preferred direction. Occasionally you need to be quite directive giving strong recommendations.

Case Vignette

Jennifer and Julia come into the session with a particular issue, an issue that has come up before and only been briefly discussed. Jennifer wants to adopt a child and Julia is not at all sure that she wants to do this. Further, Jennifer wants to adopt a child from Child Protective Services, meaning a child who has been in foster care because of abuse or neglect. Julia reels at the thought of feeling quite inadequate to be able to take care of such a child. Jennifer is passionate that this is what she wants for her life and is making the adoption a condition for the relationship continuing.

In previous sessions you have focused the couple on communication because the women were not able to discuss the current issue without Jennifer arguing and Julia withdrawing. They have made progress with this dynamic. Julia has been able to speak up more and Jennifer has been able to stop and listen. In this session you guide them to decide to focus on the pros and cons of adopting. With you keeping them on task, they are able to put together a good list of their concerns and their hopes. While they are making the list, Jennifer makes reference to guidelines from Child Protective Services for adopting. You need to ask for more information to understand the issues. This unbalances the discussion once again, with Jennifer doing more of the talking. Wanting to draw Julia more into the discussion, you turn to her to get more of the information, but she does not have it. So, you decide to let go of knowing some important details in order to not further unbalance the discussion. By the end of the discussion it is clear that Julia is overwhelmed. You reach out to her to help her express her fears. Jennifer then needs coaching to be supportive to Julia, given that she tends to be impatient with her. At the end you suggest that Julia learns more about the Child Protective Services guidelines herself to help her feel more in control. Julia agrees that this would help her. Thus, in this session there are some clear steps of problem-solving as well as sharing information, processing the couple's dynamics, bringing out emotions, and finding a next step to take.

Specific Types of Problem-centered Sessions

Most types of problem-solving sessions have characteristics in common. However, there are some types of problem-solving sessions worth discussing because of special challenges and features that they present. One example is a session focused on the steps of breaking up. The type of break-up session discussed under Crisis sessions below involves a break-up that happens right there in the session. Couples who decide to break up may then stay in therapy to get help to go through the break-up process more effectively than if they managed it on their own. These types of couples sessions are very different than normal Problem-centered sessions because the work usually does not include dealing with the couple's dynamics. In fact, because the couple is coming apart, the point is often to stay away from their dynamics or to help them keep their dynamics from interfering with the tasks of their separating. The primary role of the couples therapist is to keep the couple on track working through the steps of coming apart and to provide information that is helpful to the couple (for example, how to address the couple's children). Thus, as the couples therapist you may become a kind of gatekeeper. This type of session may be quite odd as you may have to, in fact, curtail some of your normal roles and impulses. At the same time, you can use your knowledge of the couple, who has most likely been in therapy with you while trying to stay together, to help them stay on task and avoid their well-worn pitfalls. In those rare instances in which the couple is able to go through a friendly break-up and wishes to remain friends, there may be some processing of their dynamics.

And what about problem-solving sessions in which one or both of the partners come from a different culture? Their understanding of what it means to work through a problem may be very different than yours or than each other's. The problem-solving skills that you have learned may be foreign to your clients. What if you are not familiar with the differences? For example, Ivan and Natasha, both from Russia, argue intensely and regularly about Ivan's parents who have arrived from Russia and are living with the couple. How they see the issues and how they go about resolving what to do may be unfamiliar to you. What do you do? You cannot learn all the subtleties of Russian thinking and Russian culture quickly enough. You do not want to impose your American values on them; values which may include finding another place for Ivan's parents to live. To be helpful to this couple you need to understand basic information about Russian attitudes and expectations about the elderly, Russian male-female roles within a couple, and Russian problem-solving methods. More and more couples therapists are called upon to work with couples with very different values, expectations, and understandings than those of the therapist. Sometimes you can ask the couple for information that you need. Sometimes you can get the information by listening carefully to their discussion. Sometimes you learn by making suggestions and asking the couple if these ideas fit with their values.

A Regression Session

Old behaviors come screeching back. Your couple has regressed into old patterns despite significant progress in the therapy. Something has triggered a regression. There are times when the couple comes in doing well and then regresses during the session because they are dealing with triggering issues. For example, Anita and Maxine had struggled with communication for many months. During the couples therapy they had learned how to listen to each other better. They were no longer attacking each other. They were tackling difficult issues and getting through them well. Each was able to own her issues when these issues came up and got in the way. Then at home they regressed into their old behaviors in an argument about where their daughter was going to go to school next year. They came into the couples session barely talking. Once in the session their old behaviors came charging out. What do you do in such a session? First you need to be careful not to make the situation worse. Then it is important to identify what has happened that pushed them back into their old patterns. You need to break the old cycle and help get the couple back on track. There are a number of ways of doing this:

1. You could take a time-out and have the couple decompress.
2. You could process what has gotten triggered for each of them.
3. You could review the skills they have learned.
4. You could ask them to start over now, using the skills they have learned.

This type of session may be an opportunity for the couple to go more deeply into the issues that re-stimulated their old pattern. Once these issues surface and are explored, the couple may be better able to appreciate the underlying issues that triggered the regression. Often couples need reassurance that they have not lost the skills they have learned and they are not back at square one. The old triggers can bring them into a place of hopelessness. In fact, when a couple has been making progress, it is often helpful to warn them that they will have times when they fall back. Knowing this helps them to be better prepared for the difficult feelings that come with a regression. It is helpful to give the couple the analogy of a spiral. They may slide backwards, but the slide is part of a loop on the spiral. They have not gone all the way back to the beginning even though they may feel like they have. In fact, learning the skills of coming out of a backslide is an important step in building their confidence in their learning.

This type of session can be frustrating or discouraging, not only for the couple but also for you the therapist. Even though you know most couples have regressions, it can be startling when it is right there in front of you. You may need to go back into some old roles from previous sessions in order to guide the couple. Sometimes the old strategies do not help and right on the spot you need to scramble to find some new ways of working. These types of sessions can be exhausting.

A Holding Session

Sometimes a couple just needs to be held. They are going through a tough time. They are facing something difficult. They just need to talk. June and Garth have held the line with their 22-year-old and have asked him to leave the house. Carrie is facing surgery and she and Amy are worried. Your role is not to suggest, not to solve, not to move things forward, not to provide insights. It is to hold the couple because they need nurturance and support.

Perhaps the couple is angry and upset. Perhaps they are learning to share these emotions with each other. You may need to be witness to their interactions and to provide a safe place. This too is holding. Providing a save container for the couple is holding. David Schnarch (1991) writes about therapy as a crucible. A crucible is a vessel within which a chemical reaction takes place. The vessel itself remains intact.

Sometimes a couple runs the session themselves. Applying skills they have learned, they have a discussion in which they work out an issue on their own. You decide to sit back and watch as they do their work. This is a type of Holding Session also. At some point you may join in in order to praise their work and point out the positive interactions/problem-solving that they have just done on their own. Couples often love this. They will smile with pride as you reinforce their good work. These sessions are a joy.

Holding is something couples therapists do throughout couple therapy. What is being discussed here is a session in which holding is the predominant action that the therapist is doing. These types of sessions are indeed special and often quite moving.

How do you know when a couple needs a Holding Session?

1 When they are going through something difficult and just need to give voice to their experience.
2 When the couple needs to lean on you as a support.
3 When they need to work out something on their own and are doing their work right there.
4 When they have developed the skills to conduct the session themselves, but still need you as the container.

Case Vignette

As the session develops Donald and Melvin are talking about a discussion they had after the last difficult therapy session, and Donald starts sharing the work he is doing in his individual therapy. He says he has come to realize that one of the qualities Melvin has that annoys him is actually quite helpful for them as a couple. He goes on to say that Melvin's strong organization skills, which sometimes drive him crazy, actually help them as a couple to handle their life more effectively. If he were on his own, things would not get done as well. Melvin sits in amazement as he hears Donald. When Donald is done, Melvin takes a deep breath and thanks Donald. He says he is moved by what Donald is sharing. You stay quiet as Melvin is silent for a minute. Then Melvin starts to own how he can be harsh with Donald when Donald is scattered and disorganized. As Melvin continues, you smile inside seeing a wonderful moment unfolding in front of you. You settle into holding the space for this couple to be vulnerable and open. You wait for the right time to smile outwardly and give praise to these two men for their courage in owning their parts and sharing this with each other.

13
Special Types of Couples Therapy Sessions

What do you do when faced with parenting issues or the effects on a couple of different cultural backgrounds? Some sessions present specific types of challenges that require careful and thoughtful guidance from you as the therapist. It is important to know what these challenges are and to be ready to handle them in the session. For example, what do you do when the focus of a session is primarily on one member of the couple? What do you do when faced with compliant behavior that seems inauthentic? This section tackles special types of sessions. The list of such sessions could be quite long. The reader is encouraged to think of more examples of such sessions beyond what is presented here.

Focusing on One Partner

What if the focus of a couples session is more on one partner than on the other? This can be tricky because of the possibility of imbalance in the couples therapy. Most often the sessions need to be fairly balanced. The focus of the couples therapy is the system of the couple, not on either of the two individuals alone. Thus, even when one person does become the focus, it is important to tie this work back into the couple work. When would it be appropriate for a particular couples session to focus more on one partner?

1. When it is clear that one partner's issue is blocking the progress of the couple, for example, one partner's alcohol abuse, one partner's erectile dysfunction, etc.
2. When one partner is particularly upset in a given session.
3. When one partner is having difficulty with the therapy or the therapist.
4. When one partner needs extra support.
5. When one partner is disruptive in the session.
6. When one partner has betrayed the other partner.
7. When one partner is part of the way out of the door of the relationship.
8. When one partner is having health issues.
9. When one partner is in crisis.

The goals of focusing more on one partner might include looking at the impact of that person's issues on the relationship, handling that person's emotions, answering that person's questions, and/or dealing with that partner's resistance. Zilbergeld (1995) describes a case of working with a couple where there was a critical and demanding partner. In one session he decided to give feedback to this partner about her impact on the relationship and her husband's erectile issues. It is a fascinating case in which he deftly works to give feedback to the wife in a way that she can accept, while also freeing the husband to speak his feelings. Greenan (2010) describes working with one of the partners in a session with a gay male couple. He chooses to work with this partner because, "Roberto was the more emotionally activated of the two" (p. 103). Greenan instructs the other partner to, "listen to see if you can better understand where Roberto's feelings may be coming from" (p. 103). Addison and Thomas (2010) describe a couples session in which the therapist takes on the husband in the couple about his overtly sexist remarks during the session. Addison directly confronts the husband describing how his saying that women are like bitches is offensive to her, the therapist. She then uses this to process the couple's conflicts. It is a risky strategy that Addison uses skillfully.

Yet there are circumstances in which it may, in fact, be important for the session to *not* focus on one of the partners for any of the following reasons:

1. If this focus could significantly unbalance the therapy.
2. If it is not safe in the relationship for this partner to be the focus. For example, the other partner would use this focus to make the partner wrong/at fault.
3. If the partner focused on would conclude that he/she is the problem in the relationship.
4. If the other partner would feel resentful, off the hook, anxious, jealous, etc.
5. If the other partner's issues are an important contributor or exacerbation to the partner's issues. For example, perhaps Mary's frequent put-downs of Frank contribute to his erectile issue.
6. If either partner is emotionally unstable and could not handle such a focus.
7. If such a focus would create issues for either partner with the therapist. For example, one partner might see the therapist as more on the other's side.

When working with a couple in which one partner has betrayed the other, for example, by having an affair, it can be difficult not to focus each session on the behavior of the betrayer or the feelings of the betrayed partner. Yet, it is important to attend to the feelings and needs of the other partner at some point in the session.

If one partner does become the focus of a session, it is often important to balance that out by focusing more on the other partner in the next session. It may be helpful for the therapist to alert the couple that she wants to balance the therapy by giving time to the other partner next time. Still in any given session it is important for the therapist to bring the other partner into the discussion during the session. The therapist needs to process this partner's perspective and feelings. Then the therapist needs to put the work of the session into the context of the relationship issues and dynamics. McCrady and Epstein (2015) write about working with couples in which one person has an alcohol issue. They discuss the delicate balance of working with the individual's issue and the couple.

Case Vignette

Julian is furious that he has found yet another email message from his wife Juanita to Geraldo, the man with whom she had been intimately involved for a year. Juanita had cut off the relationship with Geraldo and had assured Julian that there was no further contact. In the session Juanita is defensive at first, insisting that the email message was necessary because Geraldo is a colleague at work. Julian has copied the email and produces it with a flourish during the session. Juanita breaks down in tears, describing how lonely she feels in the marriage, how Julian is never home, and how she craves attention and affection. As the therapist you recognize that this is a breakthrough for Juanita who, until now, has been detached and defensive. You work with Juanita to open further to Julian by telling him her vulnerable feelings. You watch Julian carefully to see if he is ready to receive Juanita's opening up. He appears relieved to see her become vulnerable. Toward the end of the session you are careful to give time to Julian to talk about his reaction to Juanita's feelings, to talk about his own feelings about the marriage, and to check in with them both about how they would handle what has happened in the session later during the week. You are concerned that Julian will feel that Juanita has turned the blame for the affair on him.

Talking Through the Therapist

Joe is talking to you. Catherine is talking to you. They are not talking to each other. Sometimes this is an effective type of session. They can say things to you, even with the other one in the room, which they cannot say to each other. Why? Talking to you can ratchet down the intensity. It can keep a session from exploding. Talking to you can mean talking more responsibly, more thoughtfully, and/or with more perspective. It can help couples practice good communication skills. Talking with you can be safer and allow more emotional and vulnerable material to emerge. As couples therapists we want the partners to talk to each other. Yet, some sessions work better when the partners talk to you. Minuchin and Nichols (1998) recount a session in which the therapist has the couple talk to Minuchin because, "they still weren't ready to talk to each other without slipping into attack and defense" (p. 115).

Sometimes this type of session emerges because the partners themselves chose to talk with you. Sometimes they emerge because you are drawing out one person and then you turn to focus on the other person. Often these sessions are not planned. As they unfold, you realize that what is happening is helping the couple. Usually at some point you have the partners turn to say some of the things they have said to you to each other. This is a crucial point because what comes out when talking to each other could be quite different, causing the gain of what has happened when each talked to you to be lost. You need to gauge when and if to take the session in this direction.

Case Vignette

Carefully, thoughtfully, you the therapist draw Tareq out. Because he is talking to you and not to Layla, he is opening up emotions and vulnerabilities that would not have otherwise emerged. He is talking about how ashamed he feels of how he has hurt Layla through his lying and porn use. In his arguments with Layla he is usually defensive, in part because she becomes attacking. Tareq admits that he feels horrible about himself because of how he has hurt Layla. He's never admitted this to Layla. You are very careful about whether and when to have him speak directly to Layla. You notice that Layla's eyes have softened and she is listening intently. You judge that she can respond supportively, but you are not sure that she can do this directly to Tareq. So, you then have her talk to you rather than Tareq about what she is experiencing. Her eyes well up as she talks about how meaningful it is to her to hear Tareq admit to these things. She then gives an opening to talk about her own pain. You again determine whether it would be helpful for Tareq to hear this right now. Tareq is looking at Layla intently, so you go ahead with drawing Layla out. She expresses her deep pain that underlies her verbal attacks on him. You softly and compassionately express concern for how much pain they are both experiencing. You express the hope that they can be closer for having heard each other. They look at each other and smile.

In order to conduct a session like this, you need to see an opening in the partner who might begin the sharing. Sometimes you may know this ahead of time. Sometimes you may see the opening in the session. And sometimes the opening may come as a surprise. As you begin to see if the door will crack open, you need to tread carefully to see if the partner will allow you in. You also need to keep in mind that this partner is exposing him-/herself in front of the other partner. Through questions, reflective listening, supportive feedback, and emotional support you invite the partner to open up to deeper feelings than what is apparent. You are providing the safety for the sharing partner to be able to open up.

Susan Johnson (2011) describes a session in which the therapist first draws out the husband's feelings about coming home after doing military service. He shares his feelings with the therapist. The therapist then asks the husband to share these feelings with his wife. As a result, they are able to come closer.

A variation of the couple talking through you is you talking for them. You voice the partner's feelings and viewpoints in a way that opens up understanding and compassion for each other. Wile (2011) describes this technique in his chapter on Collaborative Couple Therapy. He gives examples from specific therapy sessions with a couple. He quotes himself in a session saying:

> Okay, Alice, so you're saying—I'll add a few things and see what you think, "Joe, maybe I should just be grateful that you agreed to come, and I am grateful, but I am not thinking of that right now. What I'm thinking about is how angry I am . . ." And Joe you're saying, "Okay sure, I gave you a tough time . . ."
>
> (p. 309)

Wile centers the session on this process of speaking for the partners. Alice and Joe had been:

> pressing their own points without acknowledging what the other is saying, which is what keeps the argument going. So I try to do some acknowledging for them and, in the process guess at their leading-edge feelings.
>
> (p. 309)

Couples Therapy Through Individual Sessions

Imagine doing couples therapy by seeing each of the partners for separate sessions. How does this work? It is not unusual for a couples therapist to see each partner separately for a session or two. But ongoing separate sessions? This does not happen often and for good reason. There are obvious pitfalls to this approach. What do you as the therapist do about secrets that may emerge? How do you handle what each partner says to the other one about what you said during their individual session? One partner may skew your words to sound like you are taking sides. But first is the question, why would doing this even be indicated/helpful? Here are some circumstances under which time-limited or situation-determined separate sessions could be helpful. In each of these situations the "client" remains the couple. These sessions are not the same as individual therapy.

1 Each person needs time to air his/her concerns and gain a perspective that he/she cannot get with the other person in the room.
2 The couple has reached a point at which they are going over and over the same points without gaining any understanding of each other. They cannot talk to each other.
3 The couple has reached a point at which they need to accept their differences and each is having difficulty doing so.
4 Each person needs some separate psychoeducation about an issue because they are unable to learn together.
5 The individuals need help preparing to be able to work together (Epstein and Baucom, 2002).

How do you as the couples therapist run an individual session that is couples therapy? Very carefully. First and foremost you need to keep in mind that anything you say may be repeated to the partner. Thus, you do not run the session as you would an individual therapy session in which your alliance is with that one person. You alliance remains with the couple. You need to be very careful not to say anything that appears to take sides. Keeping these things in mind means you have to double-think what you say and what direction the session takes. Yet, even if you are very careful, one partner may misconstrue what you said or did when describing to the other partner what happened in his/her session. If this is likely to happen, then this approach is not recommended. The goal of the separate session is to help the couple by helping the partner in front of you to gain more understanding, vent feelings, find new behaviors, and/or come to more acceptance of the "unsolvable" problems (Gottman, 1999). While you are talking to this one partner, you are holding the presence of the couple in the room. This may be a new experience for this partner—to think in terms of "me" in the context of "we." You bring this presence to the individual helping him/her to talk about his/her concerns and feelings in the context of the relationship. You do this by framing what you say in the couple context. For example, you might say, "Let's look at how you can more effectively talk with your wife about your sexual frustrations."

Some of the approaches you may take in this separate session include: supporting the partner's feelings while not taking sides, helping the partner understand their reactions and behaviors within the couple, teaching some specific skills such as communication skills, helping the partner find ways to meet the couple's agreements, and supporting the partner in working through loss of some expectations that won't be met. Atkinson (2010) describes specific sessions, working with a couple individually. With each partner he addressed his/her blaming behavior and worked with him/her to learn to take responsibility for his/her own role in the couple. When the couple came back together, they had a breakthrough of understanding and emotions. Schlanger (2011) also describes working with a couple primarily through separate individual sessions.

Another variation of this approach is seeing one of the partners only for individual sessions. How is this possible without creating an imbalance in the couples therapy? Usually this is not recommended because of the many pitfalls this can create. These pitfalls are basically the same as those in the above type of session, yet more so. So when would this even be appropriate? Primarily this would be done when one of the partners has a clear issue that needs to be addressed to help with couple therapy. Thus, if a woman is experiencing lack of sexual desire and her wife wants to be able to be sexual, it may help to see the woman with low desire for some individual sessions. Often it is more appropriate to refer the woman to an individual therapist, especially if she requires some longer-term work. However, it could be helpful for her to do some short-term sessions with you as the couples therapist since you know the partner and the couple. This kind of work can only be done if the couple is solid enough as a couple and if the partner is solid enough as a person so that the possible imbalances do not undermine the couple therapy.

Case Vignette

Rachel has little interest in sex. Wanda is understanding, but wants to see the two of them regain some of their sexual life. Wanda and Rachel agree that Rachel's main block to her sexuality is her conservative religious upbringing. Wanda is willing to see her own role in the issues and wants to be part of working together to change their sexual patterns. It is agreed that Rachel will see you the couples therapist for three sessions to work on her sexual inhibitions. In each of these three sessions you are careful to connect Rachel's issues with the couple and to reinforce Rachel's courage for doing this work. The focus of each session is working on the negative messages she learned about sexuality plus developing positive feelings about sex. You also process with Rachel the conversations she has with Wanda after each individual session. You do this to keep the individual sessions within the context of the couple. When the couple resumes couples therapy, you spend some time drawing Rachel's individual sessions into the couple work. Rachel is glad that she has insights she can share with Wanda and Wanda is relieved. If you see that Rachel needs deeper, more long-term work on her sexuality, you will refer her to another therapist for individual work.

An Outside Event Session

An external event has just happened that your couple cannot ignore. It may or may not be about something that is part of the couples therapy. The couple comes into the session and one or both of them can only focus on what has happened because it is so powerful in his/her or their lives. The couple may even want to spend the session on their couple work and may try, but the event, the issues around it, and the feelings are too strong to focus elsewhere. These experiences can take your breath away. They can be raw and fresh in the couple's life. Yet, as the couples therapist you may be concerned that talking about this event is not really doing couples therapy. Yet you need to respond to where the couple is when they are sitting in front of you. Processing what has happened may be the only option, given its effects, and it could be helpful for the couples therapy overall.

Examples of such outside issues include illness in the couple's family, upheavals at one of the partner's jobs, disruptions at the children's school, etc. These are issues that often affect the couple's life not only now, but going forward. Your job as the therapist may be to listen and support, draw out feelings, and provide some direction or information. You may need to provide some stability for your couple as they go through something difficult and emotional. The session may be one of providing them with some relief as they describe what has happened and what they are experiencing. Your role as the therapist may be quite different than the role you usually take in this couple's therapy. This may take some adjustment on your part. For example, you may normally be fairly directive with a particular couple. Now, given the circumstances, you may need to back off and primarily listen. Or you may be more process-oriented with a couple, but now you need to give some information to help.

The event may stir up some of the issues within the couple that also need to be addressed. Sometimes these issues would be best put aside for this session. Other times they cannot be ignored. Your work then may be to tie in what is happening with the issues of the couples therapy. Perhaps how they are coping with this event relates to how they function as a couple. Or perhaps some of the skills they have been learning in couples therapy can help them better handle the situation. Often when a strong external event occurs in a couple's life, it does affect the partners as a couple.

Not all external events that need attention are upsetting events. Positive events may be compelling and require attention and processing. For example, a child has been admitted to a great college, but it is across the country. Or the wife has been offered a wonderful new job promotion that she needs to respond to within a week. Amidst the celebrating, the couple needs to consider the ramifications of this new event.

Case Vignette

Prior to Max's and Cassandra's couples session, Max has learned that his mother has discovered that his father has been having an affair. His mother is very upset and is considering leaving his father. She is calling Max and confiding in him. Max and Cassandra are both upset about the situation. Their emotions are running high. Each has a different idea about how Max should handle his parents. Cassandra wants Max to call his father and confront him. Max wants both to find a way out of his parents' issues and to stop his mother from putting him in the middle. To add to the situation, Cassandra has had issues with Max's relationship with a woman coworker in the past. The air in the session is thick. As the therapist you focus the session first on what has happened, getting the events clear. You listen carefully to both partners. Then you focus on Max's feelings about his parents' situation and his position. Since this is Max's family, you feel that Max needs the most support and you want to model to Cassandra how to listen and support Max rather than to add in her own agenda right away. Once Max has expressed his concerns and emotions, you turn to Cassandra and help her to focus on her feelings rather than on what Max should do. By then, both are calmer. You then move to helping the couple explore their options and to work together as a team. You decide not to bring up the couple's history at this point because the immediate situation needs to be addressed. However, you make a mental note to come back to this possibly next time.

Parenting

When a couple has children, their couple issues may well spill over into their parenting. In addition, children have issues of their own which can affect how the couple parents. Sessions on parenting are different than most other sessions because they involve a third person; a third person for whom the partners are responsible. There are other such situations that involve a third person, such as issues with an employee or an elderly parent. But, often in these situations one partner has more responsibility than the other, the third person does not live in the house with the couple and the time commitment to the third person is less. Parents are responsible for their children's development from birth into adulthood. Parents come from different families of origin with different expectations and values. It is no wonder that parents often have quite different ideas about child-rearing. Couples come together and fall in love because of how they feel about each other and not usually because of how they imagine the other as a parent.

A session on parenting is often quite charged. The stakes are high. The couple may be full of anxiety, uncertainty, blame, and frustration. As the therapist you come to the session with your own beliefs about parenting that stem from your own upbringing, possible role as a parent, and your training as a mental health professional. Your role in a parenting session may be not only as a facilitator but also as a teacher. When do you play which role? Your primary role remains the couples therapist. If there are serious issues with the couple's child/children, you would refer them to a child specialist. Often in a session on parenting, your role is to help the parents work through their concerns or differences and look at their options using the session as a Problem-centered session. How a particular session on parenting unfolds, however, depends on many factors. For example, a Parenting session may become an Emotive session, a Teaching session, or a Crisis session. Parenting issues are usually couples issues. Partners play out their couple issues through the dynamics with their children. Unfortunately, children often get caught in the middle. The children's issues are therefore often a reflection of the couple's issues. Dickerson and Crockett (2010) describe a couples session in which a husband and wife deal with their own dynamics through a discussion of putting their children to bed.

One of the factors that makes a Parenting session different is that at some point in the session there is often a discussion about what to do about the child, especially if there is an immediate concern such as Sandy has been discovered smoking marijuana or Mark has stolen money at school. It may be tempting and, at times, necessary for you to intervene on behalf of the child speaking for the child's interests. The couple may need direct guidance from you. Giving "advice" is not what we are "supposed" to do. And yet, the situation may not be able to wait for the couple to work through what to do. Plus, they may not have the capacity or the knowledge they need. You may need to say something such as, "It seems you need to set some limits," or, "You need to talk with your child." It is quite tricky to be able to do this and remain the couples therapist. Sometimes, in fact, your taking this role can help the couple to come together as a team. Your intervention allows them to stop arguing with each other and, through you, to see the greater picture.

When a couple with children is going through a separation or divorce, parenting is a prime issue. As you guide the couple through the process of coming apart, you will likely have sessions on parenting. Your main role may be to educate the couple about co-parenting. Emery and Sbarra (2002) write about the importance of parent education for the wellbeing of the children in a divorce situation.

Cultural background can affect many aspects of a couple's life. Parenting style is particularly affected by one's background. Couples from other countries living here in the US may have very different beliefs about child-rearing than those of the couples therapist. In a session on parenting, a couples therapist needs to ask about and be respectful of a couple's beliefs and values, while at the same time not abandoning his/her own training in effective parenting. This can be quite tricky to balance.

Case Vignette

Enrico and Maria's 14-year-old Marco is running circles around them. He often smells of marijuana, comes home late, and demands new this and new that. Maria is the heavy, often attempting to set limits on Marco while Enrico is often giving in to Marco and buying him a new phone, new sneakers, etc. Maria has a hard time standing up to Enrico, often saying nothing as he undermines her parenting efforts. Marco has recently caused a small fire in his room, lighting up a joint. This pushes Maria over the edge. In a couples session she finally erupts in anger over Enrico's lack of boundaries with Marco and his not backing up her parenting efforts. He is quite taken aback. As the therapist, you first help Maria with her anger, supporting her to express it in a responsible way. You then process Enrico's dismay, helping him to see Maria's concerns. At the same time you have heard enough about Marco to see that he is on a trajectory of trouble. You feel it is important to guide the couple to some effective limit-setting before Marco causes considerable damage. You then spend time alerting them to the risks you see in Marco's behavior, coaching them on the need for limits, and making suggestions about how to deal with the fire situation. Given Enrico's Puerto Rican heritage, you believe that Enrico might particularly react to two women "telling him what to do." Recognizing the possibility that Enrico could feel ganged up on, you then work with Enrico supporting the importance of his role as a father.

A Multicultural Session

What do you do when issues of culture become the focus of the session? For example, Benyamin expects his wife Hannah to have sex with him each Friday night because it is Shabbat. Benyamin and Hannah are Orthodox Jews who deeply hold to their traditions. In their faith couples are expected to have sex as a meaningful part of the observance of Shabbat. Hannah was molested as a child and experiences sex as violating and unfulfilling. Yet, she wants to honor her beliefs. At the same time masturbation is not allowed, making this not an option for Benyamin's sexual needs. Imagine that you as their couples therapist are not Orthodox Jewish and are torn between wanting to be respectful of the couple's beliefs and seeing the need for some intervention to help Hannah not continue to experience sex as traumatizing. You feel wedged into a difficult corner, wanting to support Hannah and Benyamin. In a session such as this you must first assess how much your own biases and training are affecting your responses to the couple. Weeks et al. (2005) discuss this issue and how it can affect the therapy. You need to have an understanding of what to do when you see that your own values color your responses. You also need to assess how open the couple is to looking at issues that may conflict with their values. For example, how much do you educate the couple about trauma? Is the couple open to looking at modes of sexual interaction that might be less upsetting to Hannah yet still fulfilling for Benyamin? Sometimes the best route to take is to put the conflict on the table and discuss the different values openly. This may be particularly true when each of the partners is from a different culture, creating conflict between them.

When is it appropriate for the session to focus on cultural issues?

1 When, as with Hannah and Benymin, the couple is dealing with an issue in which their cultural values play an important role.

2 When cultural communication issues are affecting the session, i.e. language issues, cultural style, and meaning of communication.
3 When there are cultural issues that affect the couple's relationship with you.
4 When there is something important that you need to know about the couple's culture that affects the session.
5 When there are differing cultural beliefs causing issues between the partners.

Killian (2015) describes working with a couple in which the woman was Iranian and the man was American of mixed heritage. In one session the therapist works with the couple on how their "wedding could be a Christian-Muslim, North American-Persian fusion" (p. 525). The therapist helps the couple come up with a plan that feels comfortable for each partner.

One of the risks of raising cultural issues is the couple's sensitivity about such issues being discussed. They may be reluctant to discuss these issues and/or feel patronized by such a discussion. They may feel impatient with focusing on issues they think are not relevant.

Case Vignette

"He's trying to control me again!" Katerina reacts strongly when she sees Jonathan telling her what to do. She feels ordered around. Jonathan denies doing any such ordering. He says he is just expressing his needs. As their couples therapist you have noted in previous sessions that Jonathan could come across as quite definitive about what he thinks Katerina should be doing, especially in keeping up the house and their animals. The couple comes into a session with Katerina fuming. "He's at it again. Telling me what to do. 'Do this! Do that. Take the dog out. Clean the cat box.'" Jonathan reacts strongly saying he is *not* ordering her around. You decide to explore the origins of Katerina's reactivity. Katerina describes growing up in a former Eastern Soviet bloc country with an authoritarian regime. Whenever a high-level military commander came through town, which seemed to be often, all the families would be ushered quickly out of their homes into the street. They then had to stand at attention and salute the officer. This memory sparks a fuller discussion between the two partners about the differences in their childhood experiences. Jonathan was raised in a comfortable American suburb. You help Jonathan see how his experience of growing up is so vastly different than Katerina's experience. Katerina is able to tell Jonathan how her experiences make her very reactive to being told what to do. A light goes off for Jonathan helping him to see how his tone and demands tap into upsetting memories for Katerina. You explore with the couple how the trauma of Katerina's childhood experience gets triggered within the relationship, helping Jonathan to see and understand the vast differences between his childhood and hers.

A "False" Session

The couple is saying all the right things, but . . . you do not believe a word of it. Each is talking in what seems like a thoughtful and insightful way. "I know my behavior is childish and I have to act more grown-up." Or, "I can see that my anger is hurtful and I have to get better control of it." Yet you know that a lighted match would send them up in flames at a moment's notice. What do you do? Do you let them continue on in what seems like a false way? Do you stop them and redirect the session to some more real emotions? Are they lying or just being good clients, saying what you might want to hear? Are they really integrating what they have learned? Are they trying out new behaviors? In the session the couple continues on like this. You get antsy, maybe even annoyed. The central issue in a session like this is how do you guide this couple to something meaningful when what they are doing seems empty, even phony? First you need to determine what it is that they are doing. Which of the above possibilities is what is going on? Depending upon your answer, you might do any of the following:

1 If you think they are being false or lying, you might call them on it or ask what is going on because something doesn't seem right.
2 If you think they are learning from the words they are saying, you might take this learning to a deeper level, expanding it, applying it to their issues, and opening up emotions (very carefully lest a fire ignite).

3 If you think they are trying on new behaviors, you might guide them to do something that applies the new behaviors more meaningfully, such as turning toward each other and saying these statements to the other. You might also suggest ways for them to apply these behaviors in situations outside the session.
4 If you are unsure what is going on, you might note that their behaviors seem new and positive (giving them the benefit of the doubt) and you would like to understand how they came to these insights. Could they share this?
5 If you think that what they are saying is fairly empty and/or compliant and/or avoidant, you might acknowledge their thoughts in a positive way and then redirect the session to a different issue.
6 If you think that what they are saying could be a kind of breakthrough, you need to carefully guide them toward something more connected to themselves and their feelings. This can be treacherous or slippery. You could lose them easily.

These types of sessions are tricky. They may seem unreal. How can this couple be talking like this when they are usually at each other's throats? These types of sessions call on your intuition and your "felt-sense" of what is going on, based on your knowledge of the couple and your own deeper knowing. Some of the clues for you may come from your body. Do you feel antsy, tired, energized, tense? Are your alert signals going off?

Case Vignette

Pam and Isaiah are usually arguing and sniping. You as the therapist are often pulling them apart (so to speak) and helping them to sort out what led to the current fight and to better manage interacting. But today they are calmer. Pam seems to have taken your advice and is talking about her need to control her anger more. She talks about how hard she can be on Isaiah. Isaiah then talks about how he gets resentful when Pam asks him to help out and he thinks she is asking too much. He goes on to say he then retaliates by secretly doing what he wants. He says he knows this is not a good thing. You wonder what has brought about these flashes of insight and owning of responsibility. You are skeptical of their motives.

You have not heard them talk like this ever before, even though you have been diligently working with them to own their contributions to their inflammatory outbursts. You decide to tell them that you are seeing new positive behaviors on their part. You ask them what has led them to this place. Isaiah says he is tired of how they interact. Pam says she is taking to heart what you have been saying to her. You wonder. You ask them to elaborate more. Isaiah says that over the weekend they were with some friends who argue and blame, just like the two of them. Seeing themselves in their friends, he felt sick about how he and Pam treat each other. Pam says that her work with her individual therapist is helping her control herself better. Thinking that there is some true impetus behind their behaviors, you decide to try to build on these new behaviors by having them talk about how they can incorporate their self reflections into their behaviors during the week coming up. At the same time, you recognize that Pam and Isaiah will likely slide back into old behaviors before you see them next.

14
Deeper Couples Therapy Sessions

Emotions are touched. Change happens in front of your eyes. Heart-wrenching experiences are shared. These are the sessions that are deeply moving and often gratifying. They can be difficult to handle, but often in a way that really allows you to use your finest skills. You may be drained afterwards, yet often fulfilled. These are among the sessions that you most remember, often years later. Something in you is moved as the couple works through these deep issues and feelings.

An Emotive Session

Shala is sobbing. Garrett is yelling. Couples therapy sessions are often emotional. Arguing, crying, blaming, accusing, and shaking—signs of deep emotion—occur frequently. At times these emotions are helpful and at times they are not. There are certainly times when you as the therapist need to guide one or both partners away from emotions to some form of containment and understanding. An Emotive session, however, is one in which you guide one or both of the partners toward the expression of emotions. The purpose of an Emotive session is to open up and deepen the connection between the partners.

Case Vignette

Alex has recently asked Melanie to marry him. In a weekend of joy they have celebrated with their families. Their coming together is particularly poignant for them and for their families who had imagined that each of them would not find a life-long partner given that each had been single for years and were in their forties. In Alex and Melanie's recounting of their weekend, signs of fears are emerging from each of them. After giving space for their joy, you encourage each to speak of their fears. You have them each take tentative steps toward expressing their fears while you are also checking to see if the other can receive the fears. The pacing is delicate and poignant. Alex is the first to open up with his tears, describing how afraid he is that Melanie will eventually run away from his dark side. Melanie then joins in, telling how she has always imagined that no one would really want her. Each is sharing feelings that the other has not yet heard. Both are surprised and very supportive of the other.

Emotive sessions such as this one require very careful tracking of what is happening right there in the room. As the couples therapist you need to be very present and supportive to the couple. You need to note the partners' body language often using it to encourage the emotions to emerge ("Breathe more deeply into the feeling," "Keep drumming your fingers on the chair," "Stay with your emotion"). You need to direct what is happening, sometimes asking one partner to back off to make room for the emerging emotion in the other. This can be delicate work, requiring exquisite timing and sensitivity. Part of the timing is watching the clock to make sure there is enough time to encourage the emotions to emerge and to have a period of winding down from the emotions. You are continually assessing how deeply the emoting partner/s can and will go into the emotions, what it will take to bring out the emotions, whether the way the emotions are emerging is appropriate, what the effect on the partners will be, and what the ramifications of these emotions will be after the session. These sessions are often the most powerful and touching in couple work. They are often the sessions that have the most impact on the process of the couple changing. Susan Johnson (2015, p. 122) describes an emotional session in a case study. In a session Susan works with the wife to let out pent-up feelings she does not express. Through careful work the wife is able to admit through her tears that she is terrified that she is not enough for her husband.

Because the emotions that emerge often touch you as the therapist, you need to decide how best to handle your own emotions. Do you show your emotions or contain them? Do you share how you may have been touched? It can be particularly meaningful to the couple to see that their work has affected you.

Indications that an Emotive session is or could be developing include:

1. Strong body language, suggesting emotions.
2. A feeling of tension between the partners.
3. The presence of a deep issue.
4. A connection between the current issues and either or both of the partners' past issues.
5. Strong possible consequences to the issue being discussed, i.e. a high-stakes issue.
6. A buildup of unexpressed emotions over time.
7. Readiness of one or both partners to open up deeper emotions.

Goldman and Greenberg (2010) describe a case in which Goldman works with the strong emotions that the partners are experiencing. The case is particularly helpful because it gives actual dialogue from sessions. In one particular session Goldman is working with the wife's anger and hurt. She is speaking to the wife saying, "And it (being angry) is unpleasant . . . and yet you are angry. Sometimes you are really angry" (p. 272). As a result of the wife expressing her anger, she is able to speak up for her needs and her husband is reassured because he sees her as being more honest. Deeper issues emerge and tensions are relieved (points 3 and 6 above). The case and the session illustrate how powerful Emotive sessions can be and how they can be a catalyst for change in a couple.

Touching Deep Wounds

This is tender work. Kathleen may be in tears not only because she feels rejected by Sam but also because she experienced hurtful rejection within her family. In the multicultural case above, Jonathan's tone and demands evoked deep feelings in Katerina because of her experience growing up in a totalitarian regime. Couples issues can often tap into deeper wells of unhealed issues and emotion. We often bring our greatest vulnerabilities and needs into our intimate relationships. These needs and vulnerabilities may go back to our previous hurts and disappointments. Most couples work at some point touches on our histories.

Sometimes the couples work triggers deeper wounds right there in the couples session. It can then be very helpful for the couples therapist to bring the deeper issues out and help the partners process the connection to their current couple's dilemmas.

Sessions including deeper wounds can be of various types:

1 An emotional sharing in which the partner/s experiences the wound right in the room.
2 Insightful reflection about the wounds without the strong emotions.
3 Discussion of the wounds in a way that deepens the couple's understanding of the dynamics of their current dilemma.

A primary goal of surfacing these deeper wounds is to help the couple gain greater understanding of and empathy for each other, and therefore to deepen the connection between the partners. Another important goal is to help them move through their current issues by building this connection.

In this type of session you as the therapist need to show a deep respect for the wounds that the partner/s is sharing. It is important to be gentle, clear, and solid during this level of work. The partner/s sharing the wound is vulnerable and sometimes raw. Safety is of the utmost importance. You need to judge if, indeed, the couple is ready for such sharing and if the receiving partner will respect the sharing, not only in the session but after. If this sharing is thrown back at the sharing partner now or later, that partner will be further wounded. It is helpful to talk about this during the session.

One of the great benefits of this type of session is that uncovering the deeper wounds helps the couple to have more compassion for each other and to be less blaming of the other. When one partner understands the wounds behind the partner's reaction and, in addition, knows that the partner is willing to address these wounds, often the partners can become significantly closer. However, the risk is that the listening partner will not be understanding and will further blame the sharing partner. Then, as the couples therapist, you need to work with the listening partner to hopefully bring him/her to a more compassionate place.

One of the challenges of this type of session is that the session can become unbalanced if the focus is too much on one person. At the same time, when both people are sharing their deeper wounds, the session can become overwhelming for one or both. A further challenge can be to not get lost in the sharing of the wounds, such that the couple or one of the partners leaves in too raw a state.

Some approaches, such as object relations couples therapy (Scharff and Bagnini, 2002), focus on these deeper places, connecting what is happening currently in the couple to their childhood issues. Other approaches, such as strategic and structural therapy (Keim and Lappin, 2008), do not believe this deeper work is necessary for substantive change to take place. Some would say that this deeper work is for individual therapy and not for couples therapy. Thus, one's orientation as a therapist may determine the extent to which deeper wounds are explored as part of the couples work. Many couples therapists are eclectic in their work, drawing on deeper issues when appropriate and when needed in order to move the couple through their current dilemmas. One of the most gratifying experiences as a couples therapist is to work with the individual therapists of each partner, should they have them. In the individual work the partners do the background work that can help support their couples therapy. When appropriate, the partners can then bring this work into the couples sessions. The individual therapist might encourage his client to share this in the couples session because it can be a safe place.

For a case vignette of a session of working with deeper wounds, see the above multicultural case of Katerina and Jonathan. In fact, during the session while Katerina is describing her experience growing up in a totalitarian regime, she becomes quite emotional as she remembers being marched out of her home and forced to salute. Her fear is palpable right in the room. Jonathan has known of her history, but had no idea of the depth of its effect on Katerina. After this session, he is more able to temper his way of talking with her in order to not elicit her fears.

Schwartz Gottman (2004) in her case about an extramarital affair (discussed above under Crisis sessions) describes a session in which the husband in the couple admits that he is not as attracted to his wife as he used to be because he thinks she is too thin. The wife is stunned and angry. The therapist then works with the husband and uncovers that his wife's thinness brings back painful memories of his mother losing weight after her mastectomy. His mother then did not want to hold him anymore. Getting close to his thin wife brought up these feelings of rejection. Schwartz Gottman writes, "Frank needed to uproot his feelings, link them to their source in childhood, and separate them out from his connection to Judy. Then he could be free to embrace her in every way" (p. 62). The case shows how deeper wounds can directly affect the couple's dynamics today.

A Breakthrough Session

These sessions are the holy grail of couples therapy. After such a session a couples therapist may well say to him-/herself, "This is why I do this work." Breakthrough sessions are those in which something remarkable happens that breaks through the couple's patterns and leads to new understandings and ways of relating. These sessions can be tremendously satisfying for the therapist and most of the time for the couple. "Most of the time" is written because breakthrough sessions can rock the boat. They can be disruptive in a positive and also a disorienting way. They are often the result of hard work, commitment, and a willingness to go deep.

Case Vignette

For years Janice had been upset that Ron did not relate to her in an emotional way. He seemed detached and unconcerned. In addition, for years Janice has felt hurt that Ron had not come to the hospital the day she had a miscarriage. Before couples therapy Ron had gone to individual therapy with little result. He had learned a lot about himself and his upbringing, with little impact on the relationship. In the current couples therapy session Janice is describing the hurt and growing hopelessness she still feels about Ron's detachment. She starts to weep as she describes the day of the miscarriage. Ron looks uncharacteristically affected by her tears. He shifts around in his chair. You ask him what is happening. He says he doesn't know, but he is clearly uncomfortable. Janice stops, surprised at seeing some reaction on Ron's part. Suddenly he blurts out, "I see it," as if a blurry picture is coming into focus. He shakes his head. His tears start.

"I see myself as a child standing at the back of the kitchen. No one notices me." He hesitates. Turning to his wife, he says, "I am doing the same thing to you that they did to me! I did not pay any attention to you that day just like they did not pay any attention to me." Ron is overcome at this revelation. Now all three people in the room have tears in their eyes.

This experience changed Ron. In sessions after this he repeated to Janice to stop him if he did this to her again. It took months for Janice to trust that, indeed, this epiphany had truly changed her husband.

Ron's type of breakthrough is a "Polaroid" breakthrough. Years ago when people had Polaroid cameras, the picture would come out of the camera blank. Slowly colors and shapes would appear. At some magical point the image would appear in a comprehensible form. At that point you could see what the picture showed. For Ron there were pieces available that coalesced into a new understanding at that moment. As a couples therapist you can sometimes feel that something is in the making. There is a pull, a sense that something could emerge. The moment is delicate and must be handled carefully or it could fade just like a thought that almost comes into focus, but disappears before making itself known. Your work is to hold and direct the energy so that the breakthrough can happen. You need to be able to hold the tension, feel the direction of the emerging energy, direct the emotions and the conversation, and ward off distractions and deflections. These sessions can be riveting. You may be on the edge of your chair, reminding yourself to breathe deeply and trust your instincts. You are working to not let the potential breakthrough slide away out of view.

Hazlett (2000) describes a Breakthrough session with a couple who has "looked directly over the edge of the abyss at divorce" (p. 36). Through careful guidance by the therapist the couple is able to move from distance and anger to closeness. The breakthrough that emerges is that the wife is able to uncover that it is not the prevalent anger and critique from her husband that she fears. Rather, it is his withdrawal and absence. When he sees this, he softens and is able to let her in. Atkinson (2010) describes a Breakthrough session after seeing each partner in the couple individually for a number of sessions. Each partner reads a letter to the other. In the letters they share the ways they have hurt each other. As this unfolds, they both soften, apologize, and share deep emotions in a new way. The author writes of the session, "This was one of those sessions that therapists live for" (p. 195).

There are many kinds of Breakthrough sessions. One of the most meaningful kinds can be the above Emotive session (although Emotive sessions do not necessarily lead to breakthroughs). In addition to emotive breakthroughs, there are also insight breakthroughs. Insight breakthroughs are more cognitive in nature. Something which was not understood now comes to make sense. They involve "aha" moments for the couple. An example involves times when both partners come to understand why the other person did what they did. For example, that action that was so "wrong" now makes some sense. Usually the partners soften toward each other and are able to feel more compassion. Stendhal (2003) describes a breakthrough moment in a session. Sybil and Mariushka have been flirting with other women to enhance their sexual relationship. They discover that each of them does not like doing this and only does it for the other one so she won't be bored. In fact, they are both tired of doing this behavior. When they discover this, they both laugh uproariously. Stendhal writes, "In this breakthrough moment for Sybil and Mariushka, the truth came as a surprise and brought instant relief to them both" (p. 41).

Another type of Breakthrough session involves new information emerging—information that clarifies history, actions, motivations, etc. Perhaps one or both partners have forgotten something critical that shaped events. Perhaps one of them learns of something new and shares it. Perhaps one has been withholding important information. Couples therapists know that there is often important information that is missing in couples' narratives of their lives. As the therapist elicits the couple's narrative, he may be guiding the couple toward the ability to recall and/or share this information. When the therapist senses what may be coming, he/she needs to evaluate whether the couple is ready for the information to emerge. He/she may decide that the couple is not yet in a place to handle the information. They may need to build more skills, more trust, and more background information first.

Sometimes a partner may be waiting to divulge certain information until the therapy session because he/she wants the help of the therapist in bringing it out and/or in handling the partner's reaction. This can be very tricky if that partner is using the therapist to buffer him-/herself, to gain an ally, or to leave the therapist holding the bag.

Thus, not all Breakthrough sessions are positive. There can, indeed, be negative Breakthrough sessions. Devastating information emerges, someone falls apart, and/or time for handling the breakthrough runs out leaving someone in pieces. These sessions are not the holy grail. They are more like earthquakes. An example of a negative breakthrough includes one partner's realization that she has no sex drive because she is no longer attracted to her partner. Another example includes one partner revealing that behind his emotional absence in the relationship is the likelihood that he is losing his job. In negative Breakthrough sessions your work as the therapist may be to collect the pieces and to try to put the partners back together enough to leave. Although a negative breakthrough may precipitate a crisis, it can lead to positive change by breaking through where the couple is stuck.

Sometimes Breakthrough sessions happen without the couple realizing that there has been a breakthrough. You as the therapist then need to decide how to handle the couple's lack of awareness. You could decide to show excitement and point out what has happened. Or perhaps you could lead the couple toward discovering for themselves what has happened. Sometimes you may realize the couple is not ready to handle the breakthrough that has just happened. You may then need to ease them into a step-by-step understanding of the breakthrough and its ramifications.

Breakthroughs can be elating for you as the therapist. You have waited for this! This is a culmination of important and perhaps slogging work that the couple has been doing. It all seems worth it. You leave the session with big deep breaths. You realize how much you have been carrying. Yet there is a lot of responsibility ahead. How will you keep the breakthrough alive and meaningful? For now, however, it is important to enjoy this moment. It is sweet and does not come often enough.

When the breakthrough is negative, it can be devastating not only to the couple, but to you. You may be caught off guard. You may be angry at one or both partners. You may feel fooled or used. You may regret the direction in which you took the session. You are probably thinking a mile a minute about where to go next. You may need to call a colleague for support and ideas.

A Turnaround Session

The couple comes into the session in one state and leaves in quite a different state. This can happen in any number of the types of sessions discussed in this section. What is specifically referred to here is the type of session in which a couple comes in angry and hostile, or sad and dispirited, or distant and alienated, and leaves closer, more connected, and warmer together. This experience during which a marked turnaround happens right then and there is a category in and of itself. As the therapist you recognize that a turnaround is what needs to happen. The couple needs to find a different state or the session will not work. It may seem like finding any kind of change will be like turning an ocean liner around. Yet, during the session something happens that allows the couple to find their way toward each other. They come in far apart and leave closer together. This type of session is different than a Breakthrough session in that it is it not as intense or as impactful for the relationship as a whole. It is in the moment. Hopefully it builds upon itself, but this will take time.

Case Vignette

Yolanda and James are barely talking. Yolanda is shooting daggers at James as she announces that he is not talking to her. James claims that Yolanda has been pounding on him all week telling him everything he is doing wrong in the relationship. At the root of this is a trip James took to London for work. London was where he had had an affair and then lied about where he been. Right before the trip Yolanda was triggered and tried to get James to be understanding about her fears. James's approach was to tell her things he would do to keep in touch: email, texting, etc. Yolanda wanted him to show empathy. James was on the defensive. In the session each describes what the other one is doing wrong. The tension is thick. As the therapist you wonder how you can get them out of their stuck and hostile positions. You take an opening from James when he says he has difficulty with empathy. You ask if James is willing to work with this now. He reluctantly agrees. You then ask him to tell Yolanda what he imagines she went through while he was on his trip. He is able to squeak out some words of understanding of her experience. Yolanda starts crying and begins to talk about her feelings rather than attacking James. There is a delicate balance between them as this unfolds. As they soften toward each other and make an emotional connection, you praise their work and help them to recognize what they have done. Each says they feel closer. At the end they leave arm in arm. You breathe a sigh of relief.

These types of sessions are very demanding. There is tension, distance, and frustration in the room. You feel the pressure to make something different happen or the session will be a bust yet you may be at a loss. You hope you can find a way to help the couple get connected. What can you do?

1. Wait for an opening to work with (as in the example).
2. Put the responsibility back on the couple to find a way to make some connection.
3. Remind the couple of prior times during which they have been able to get through similar situations back to some closeness. Remind them of how they did this.
4. Try something brand new to turn the ship around.
5. Change the ship into a row boat, i.e. help the couple shrink the tense situation into something manageable.
6. See if one of the partners will take some ownership of his/her role in the current state. Then work with this to create an opening with the other partner.

In this type of session there are a number of factors you need to weigh in order to figure out how to get a turnaround: how wedded are the partners to their positions, how much will each partner let you direct him/her, how risky is your strategy, how often has the couple been in this dilemma before, and how successful are you at producing miracles? This last question is tongue in cheek, yet a miracle may be what is needed. Clearly it is not our job to produce miracles, yet sometimes what we do in a session like this, when it works, may feel like some kind of magic.

A Celebration Session

There are two weeks until the couple's wedding. Or the couple has recently had a baby. Or one of the partners has a new job. Or their child has been accepted into college. The couple is aglow. They sit with you and talk about this special event that is happening. You wonder how to make the session productive since they are here in therapy. Do you just sit and listen? Do they want to move on and get into issues? Sometimes a couples session of celebration is just basking in the glow. The couple may just need to recount to you what has happened. You may be able to help them more fully take in and truly absorb this wonderful event. You may be able to take them more deeply into their feelings. You might tie this event into their work that contributed to this special outcome. These sessions are likely to be ones of joy and tears.

How wonderful are these sessions for you as well as the couple, particularly when the special event is in some part a result of the therapy work with you! Perhaps the couple has worked through difficult issues of intimacy and sexuality resulting in them being able to commit to getting married. Perhaps they have addressed overwhelming issues of infertility, IVF, and now their baby has arrived and mother and baby are doing well. Perhaps the couple has had great difficulty with their son through high school. Over time with the couple's help the son has rallied and has just been accepted to college. These are moments to be treasured. You can help the couple find special ways to value these times, whereas on their own they might pass through them without fully feeling their joy and accomplishment. You might suggest some ways of marking this occasion—going out to dinner, writing something to their son, taking time off, telling each other what they appreciate about each other. For example, with Daniel and Anita, whose wedding was ten days away, their couples therapist had each of them turn to the other and tell the other why they were marrying him/her. They each said things to each other that they had never said—wonderful and deep messages of love, insight, and appreciation. As a result, the couple went into their wedding day even more connected.

A Celebration session can be an opportunity to learn about the traditions and customs of your couple. Weddings, anniversaries, Bar and

Bat Mitzvahs are times when cultural and religious traditions and rituals are observed. As you listen to your couple recount and rejoice in their celebration, you can ask about and take notice of their values and beliefs through their stories.

What are the challenges of such a session?

1. The couple getting into issues that spoil the celebration.
2. One or the other partner diminishing the accomplishment.
3. One or the other partner taking the credit for the accomplishment.
4. The couple coming up against one or both partner's difficulty in celebrating, in taking in something positive, in feeling pride, in feeling good about him-/herself.
5. The fear of the road ahead dulling the joy of now.
6. The couple not knowing what to do to actually celebrate.

Some of these issues may have to be addressed during the session particularly if they are blocking celebrating. Hopefully you have already addressed these issues so that now you can help the couple put them aside and focus on feeling good.

How do you as the therapist handle such a session? Enjoy it fully. We do not get these sessions all that often. They are part of our reward for the intense and demanding work that we do. We may see a rough road ahead for the couple with their ongoing issues. For now, drink in their joy and accomplishment . . . as well as yours.

Yet there may be obstacles for you. You may feel restless during such a session. We are geared to "work" during a session. We are geared to confront difficult issues. Is celebrating a legitimate way to spend a session? Will the couple resent paying for feeling good? We need a way to understand these sessions as part of the couple's growth. We also need to explain this growth to the couple so they understand the importance of the celebrating. Couples may give you a lot of credit for being where they are. How do you accept this and also give credit back to them for their hard work? You need to be able to be gracious and not throw off the couple's appreciation of you. At the same time you need to point out that they did the work and/or that the work was a collaboration. What if they do not acknowledge your role at all? You may feel annoyed, dismissed, unappreciated. These are your feelings to handle.

Sessions such as these can be difficult for you if the event touches some similar issue in your life that did not go well or currently is not going well. While you are celebrating your couple's marriage, perhaps you are going through a divorce. While you are celebrating the couple's birth of their child, you may be taken back to your history of miscarriages. Your own disappointment and grief may bubble up, making it hard to lead this celebration.

15
Intervention Exercises

During the Full Steam Ahead period of the session, you may well use some kind of intervention exercise. The purpose of such an exercise is to help the type of session that is unfolding to work more effectively. Thus, the exercise must make sense with the type of session underway. In this book an intervention exercise is defined as specific actions that the therapist asks the couple to do in order to shift the dynamics between them and/or to help resolve an issue. Thus, an intervention exercise might directly address a communication pattern or it may help the couple resolve a problem such as how to initiate being sexual. The term "intervention exercise" is used here to distinguish it from an "intervention" which might not be something the therapist asks the couple to do. Some interventions, for example, are observations or interpretations made by the therapist. If the therapist decides on using an intervention exercise, he/she needs to think through what it will be, how it will possibly help, whether there is time to do it, and what snags might arise while using the intervention. Thus, in a Parenting session the therapist might introduce a role-playing exercise in which one of the partners plays the child while the other partner plays the parent. The goal would be for the parents to be more ready to handle what may result from a proposed approach to talking with the child. In a Problem-centered session the therapist might ask the couple to write down the pros and cons of a particular action they are considering. Thus, the intervention exercise is to serve the type of session at hand. Intervention exercises also need to fit your couple and where they are in their therapy. Brok (2011) writes:

> Try to tailor your interventions based on your accumulated knowledge of the couple's style of relating . . . and your tentative diagnostic understanding of what might be getting in the way of your couple's optimal relationship.
>
> (p. 62)

Bringing in an intervention exercise is an exciting moment. Something could change. Something could emerge. Old ways could be shattered. On the other hand the intervention exercise could fall flat and do nothing. Or, worse, it could set off something negative in the couple.

Choosing to use an intervention exercise is an art that requires skill, experience, and intuition. Some intervention exercises fit into a situation like a hand into a glove. As the therapist, you may have used the intervention exercise many times and know it will be likely to help. Other intervention exercises are a gamble that you need to weigh, often in just a few minutes or even seconds. Some intervention exercises just appear to you and you run with them. You may be starting the intervention exercise almost before knowing it. Some come as the result of you trying to find something that will help, sifting through various possibilities and then choosing one. Many schools of couples therapy include intervention exercises. Some are subtle and others rock the boat, asking the partners to try out quite new behaviors. Examples of intervention exercises include the following: magic wand from strategic/structural therapy (Keim and Lappin, 2002); reframing (Weeks et al., 2005) and constructive problem-solving (Christensen et al., 2015) from cognitive behavioral therapy; externalizing conversations, and naming the problem from narrative therapy (Freedman and Combs, 2015); and stress-reducing conversation and time-outs from Gottman's marital therapy (Feutz, 2004). Keim and Lappin (2002) discuss the use of interventions in strategic/structural therapy. They write:

> A directive is a communication by the therapist suggesting that a client experience, think, and/or behave differently. An intervention or technique is a collection of directives given to achieve a clinical goal.
>
> (p. 102)

In a case study they discuss a therapist introducing a 14-step formal negotiating process to a couple (pp. 105–106). In structural therapy the use of an intervention exercise is one of three centerpieces of the work. This step is called unbalancing. Greenan and Tunnell (2003) define the unbalancing process as follows. The therapist, "reflects what he saw the couple do to each other and then he introduces novelty to the system as he invites the couple to experiment with new behavior" (p. 139). Susan Johnson (2015) gives an overview of the core interventions used in Emotionally Focused Couple Therapy. These include replaying interactions and restructuring and shaping interactions (p. 112).

When learning about an intervention exercise from a particular therapeutic approach, couples therapists learn about how to use that particular exercise within the framework of that particular approach. Most couples therapists draw from any number of approaches and use intervention exercises that fit the couple where they are in their therapy and in the particular session at hand.

There are issues the therapist needs to consider when contemplating and using most any intervention exercise. Below are three important steps you as the couples therapist need to take into account in using an intervention exercise. The questions you need to consider are listed under each step.

1 Choosing an intervention exercise

   a) What does the couple need?
   b) What intervention exercise could help with this need?
   c) What is the goal of this possible intervention exercise?
   d) What are the steps of the intervention exercise?
   e) Does the exercise fit with the type of session unfolding?
   f) Are the partners ready and able to handle the intervention exercise?
   g) Are you the therapist comfortable with and able to handle the intervention exercise?
   h) How long will the intervention exercise take and do you have the time?
   i) Does the intervention exercise fit with the overall therapy?

j) How will the couple and you deal with the outcomes of the intervention exercise?

Keim and Lappin (2002) write of choosing an intervention, "Interventions/techniques must take into account each couple's social and therapeutic context. Specific interventions may be associated with specific problems" (p. 102).

2 Implementing the intervention exercise

a) How do you introduce the intervention exercise? Do you explain it or do you just launch into it?
b) What element of surprise do you want to have in the intervention exercise in order get around possible defenses?
c) How do you show the partners the value of the intervention exercise?
d) How do you handle doubts either member of the couple has about the exercise?
e) How do you guide the couple through the steps of the intervention exercise? How do you keep them on track in order to accomplish the goal?
f) How do you improvise to keep the intervention exercise effective?
g) How do you handle resistance to the exercise while it is happening?
h) How do you handle strong emotions that may emerge during the exercise?
i) What do you do if the exercise becomes overwhelming for either couple member?
j) How do you handle it if the exercise is not working?

3 Processing the intervention exercise

a) What steps do you use to process the intervention exercise?
b) How do you help the couple experience the desired outcome from the intervention exercise? How do you help them learn alternative or additional outcomes from the experience?

c) How do you handle any difficulty the couple has with you from the intervention exercise?
d) How do you manage any strong emotions that have resulted from the intervention exercise?
e) How do you handle any negative outcome from the intervention exercise?
f) How do you integrate the exercise into the type of session underway?
g) How do you show the partners how to integrate the experience into the overall goals of the therapy?
h) How do you bring the intervention exercise to a meaningful close?

As you consider an intervention exercise, imagine processing all of this in seconds while the session continues. Experienced couples therapists do just that. They also rely on their experience to handle outcomes that are unexpected and that they may have misjudged. New couples therapists need to take some risks based on their best judgment in order to learn. Even for experienced therapists there are always some risks and unknowns in introducing an intervention exercise. This is the nature of the work and part of what makes it fascinating and innovative.

Implementing an intervention exercise can be a challenge because of the couple's inertia. They are used to their patterns. They may not be comfortable trying something new and strange such as role-playing. You need to sell the intervention with your enthusiasm, engagement, and/or explanation. Here are some ways to engage the couple:

"I'd like to try something new that I think would help you right now. Are you game?"

"I've got an idea of how you could get out of this bind. Let me explain to you something I'd like you to try."

"I'm going to lead off with something that I think would help you. If you find it helpful, then there are some steps you can take."

Once you see an opening in the form of agreement or interest, you need to become directive, telling the couple what you want them to do.

Intervention exercises require both buy-in from the couple and leadership from the therapist.

Intervention exercises usually require close guidance through the process. Partners will often step outside of the structure of the exercises. They may be uncomfortable, they may have a different agenda, they may not know how to do such an exercise, they may resent the process, etc. As a result they may exhibit various behaviors such as talking to you when they have been instructed to talk to the other, laughing inappropriately, joking, being sarcastic, making digs at the other, saying the exercise is stupid, or saying they can't do the exercise. You need to not be easily daunted by such evasions and have ready ways to keep the partners going. You need to be quick to keep them on track or the intervention exercise may fall apart. Some of the kinds of things you might say to them include:

"I know this feels strange (contrived, pointless, uncomfortable), but stay with it for a bit longer."

"I think we are getting to something important. Let's keep going."

"After we are done, we can talk about how this seems weird (contrived, uncomfortable etc.). Let's keep going for now."

"You are doing great with this."

As the therapist you need to carefully watch how the intervention is unfolding. You may need to tweak the intervention exercise to make it more effective, to help the couple stay with it, and to make it fit with the type of session underway. One of the intervention exercises used in John Gottman's marital therapy is "the-dream-within-the-conflict" exercise. Swartz Gottman (2004) and Feutz (2004) describe using this intervention in specific sessions. It is helpful to see how the therapist guides the exercise carefully in order that the couple are able to do it and get the most out of it. Schwartz Gottman (2004) quotes her own words during an intervention as follows, "Frank, your own view seems to be sneaking in. Let me help you here. Why don't you ask Judy . . ." (p. 64). She is keeping the couple on track.

Exercises often need to be adapted. Part of being creative is changing the intervention, combining it with a different exercise, and/or becoming more involved with the exercise yourself. Sometimes you may even need to let it fall apart. An exercise that does not work may show the couple something important about the relationship. When an exercise falls apart, it is important that you process what happened that made it not work. Sometimes this discussion may lead to resuming the exercise or doing a different exercise.

Carson and Casado-Kehoe (2011) write:

> Therapists must be prepared to react in a therapeutic and professional way when interventions fall flat or elicit unexpected negative or resistant reactions in or between clients. Even these resistant or "non" experiences can be reprocessed with clients in a way that can have surprising impact on them.
>
> (p. 246)

Processing the intervention exercise is a crucial step in the process. It is not enough to just have the couple participate in the intervention exercise. Without good processing, an intervention exercise can be a waste or even harmful. There are aspects of the intervention exercise couples will not get or absorb without good processing. The partners could miss important insights. They may have important questions to ask after. Each partner needs a chance to express their feelings and insights. Processing involves helping the couple to make meaning of their experience. You need to help them understand what happened and what they can take from their experience.

In a number of the case vignettes already given throughout the book, there are examples of the therapist using an intervention exercise. For example, in the Turnaround session the case vignette describes a husband and wife arguing about a trip the husband took to a place where he had cheated on his wife. The therapist sees that the husband needs to be able to express some empathy toward his wife. The therapist then asks the husband to tell his wife what he imagines she was feeling when he went on this trip. Only then does he soften and show some empathy for her. This then turns a disastrous session around.

In the Crisis session dealing with secrets there is a case vignette with a husband revealing that his business and his finances are in real trouble. During the session the therapist, after working through some of the shock and emotions of this revelation, has the couple begin to develop a financial plan right there in the session. In both of these examples, the therapists carefully weigh the introduction of these interventions to make sure they will be appropriate, doable, and helpful.

Summary of Full Steam Ahead

This is the heart of the work. Full Steam Ahead is the time to delve into the issues and make significant headway. This section looks at how the work unfolds and at the obstacles that can get in the way. Four categories of types of sessions are discussed: Difficult sessions, Classic sessions, Special Types of sessions and Deeper sessions. Twenty-six types ofsessions are described. In addition interventions that might be used during this period are discussed. This is the prime focus of the journey.

Section VI
Pulling It Together: 35–45 Minutes

16
Introduction and "Ahas"

You have 15 minutes left to go. You are still getting into the work. Or, you are deepening the work. Or, nothing productive is happening. Or, you are herding cats. The next 10 minutes may make or break the session. When you are 35 minutes into the session you as the therapist need to start anticipating the ending of the session in earnest. What needs to be said and done? What must be said and done? Even as the work of the session is continuing, you need to be planning the denouement. Scenarios of how to pull the work together and how to find a stopping place begin to play out in your mind. These scenarios then inform what needs to happen in these last 15 minutes. How does the current issue tie back into the larger issues? How can the couple be brought down off the ledge into a calmer place? How can there be learning from what is taking place? You need to ask yourself questions such as the following: When do I start taking an active step to bring about an understanding of what is happening? How to I guide the couple to finding meaning from the session? Do I need to sew the patients up so that I do not leave them bleeding on the table? What is going to happen after they leave? The session needs closure.

This time period may be the richest part of the session if handled well. Hopefully the couple has been into the meat of the work. The circling around has happened. There has been a commitment to a direction and the couple has sunk their teeth into the work. This is the time for the work to come together. Insights are developing. Understandings are being reached. This time period may be quite gratifying when the work does come together. You as the therapist move into the important role of connecting, explaining, bringing in overviews, and helping to make sense of what is taking place. This calls on your ability to pull pieces together to form a whole. It may be like the moment during work on a jigsaw puzzle when the picture starts to become clear. The colors, the separate images, and the fragments make sense.

Because many case studies of couples therapy sessions do not describe the latter parts of the session, but rather focus on the meat of the session, there are a very limited number of available cases to draw from for these remaining 10 to 15 minutes of a session. The ones that do recount these last sections of the session, Pulling It Together, Ending and Leaving, are quite helpful and are cited here.

"AHAS"

During this period you are looking for aha moments. Sometimes they are already evident to you and maybe the couple. Sometimes you do not know what they are until they are coming out of your mouth. You start talking about the work and it comes together as you speak. You may be surprised as your thoughts unfold. Sometimes you need to go into double-think, during which you are still conducting the session while at the same time you are working out how to pull the work together. Sometimes you recognize the picture because you have seen many like it before. Even though each therapy session is different, there are patterns that become familiar.

Songs often have a structure, such as ABAB. Therapy sessions have structure also. You need to surface that structure and help the clients to see it. During this Pulling It Together period you may lead the couple back through the structure of the particular session that they are in so that they can to come to clearer insights and meaning as the session draws to a close. The aha moment can take different forms, depending on the type of therapy session that has been happening.

Often it is helpful to ask the couple some form of, "What do you take away from the work today?" The couple may have insights and understandings beyond what you are seeing. Because this is their therapy and their experience, they may know more about how to pull the work together than you. You are a team of three who have gone through this experience.

Even when it is clear to you what the picture looks like and what needs to be pulled together, it is often more helpful when the couple comes to the ahas on their own. It is indeed exciting when this happens. It builds confidence and trust between the partners when they can step back and see the big picture themselves. If they cannot get there, you may need to step in to help them.

Below is a list of different kinds of ahas that may occur during this period.

1 You and the couple together process the session in order for the couple to consolidate what they have experienced and learned.
2 You offer your summary and insights of the significance of the work in the session to deepen the couple's understanding and appreciation of their work.
3 You help the couple see how the issue of this session ties into the couple's larger issues.
4 The couple comes to see how the therapy work can be integrated into their cultural values.
5 The couple integrates a breakthrough that has occurred.
6 You help the couple make an emotional connection with each other through the work they have done.
7 The couple comes to some direction for dealing with the issue that has been discussed.

    a) They come to a better understanding of each other's viewpoint and feelings.
    b) They discuss more about what they want to learn to deal with the issue.
    c) The couple finds new resources within themselves.
    d) The couple discovers new external resources to explore.
    e) The couple develops a new plan for addressing the issues.
    f) They find a new specific action step they can agree on.

Some of the ways you might address the couple to help them integrate their work include:

"We have been discussing several ways of handling the issue. Let's see how we can work them together."

"It doesn't have to be either/or. It can be both," and, "Let's explore this."

"Do you see how you are both experiencing similar feelings and dilemmas?"

"Let's talk about how this dynamic around this issue ties in with similar dynamics in your relationship."

"Let's organize these different options that we have discussed into a plan."

Freedman and Combs (2015) recount a session of tension between a husband and wife. Through their work the wife comes to understand that the husband does, indeed, wish to be close to her. Near the end of the session the couple consolidates their work (see point 1 above) by "telling stories of closeness: reading aloud to each other, hiking together . . ." (p. 290).

Sometimes the couple may not come to an aha in the session. You may need to give them homework to facilitate some learning to happen. Minuchin and Nichols (1998) describe Minuchin saying to a couple toward the end of a session, "You both want something you're not getting . . . Attention. Genuine attention . . . Now I'm going to give you homework. I would like each of you to find some other way of getting what you want from each other" (p. 125).

Tying in Larger Issues: Aha point 3

Some of these types of ahas bear further discussion. For example, during this Pulling It Together time it may be very important to go back to a loose end or an issue from a previous session. This is especially true if that issue ties into what has been dealt with in the current session. Connecting the current issues to past work helps to provide continuity to the therapy. It provides a broader context for the work the couple has done in this current session. It will often bring insight into the work of today. This helps the couple to see the progress they are making. Without these connections the couple may not integrate the current work into their previous work. They could then repeatedly rework the issues. Freedman and Combs (2015) recount the latter part of a session in which the therapist ties the couple's work on success in their careers to their larger issue about whether they want *success* to control their relationship or whether *they* want to control and define their relationship.

CASE VIGNETTE OF POINT 3

Brad and Marta spend their session discussing their anxiety about Brad leaving his job. Brad is having difficulty using his time productively. Both are concerned about money. Brad has started taking over more of the household duties, freeing up Marta to get more of her work done. He understands how this is helpful for the family, but he is also resentful. They decide to come up with a plan for Brad's time over the next six months. They look at him having a transition and recovery period, a period to get some house projects done, and a period for his job search. Thus, the session becomes a Problem-solving session. As the last 15 minutes of the session approach, you as the therapist bring up the couple's previous difficulties in working through transitions in their lives. Marta often became quite anxious and put pressure on Brad. Brad often closed down and did not follow through on tasks. Through their therapy they have learned ways to handle these patterns and have developed some effective strategies for coping with their differences. At this point in the session, you remind them of this work in order to help them put the current work in the context of their previous work. You exclaim what a pleasure it is to see them work through a difficult issue so well. This helps to strengthen the gains from the session.

BREAKTHROUGH: AHA POINT 5

When a couple has had a Breakthrough session (see above), they are often somewhat overwhelmed even if they are joyful or relieved. Breakthroughs can change their reality. One or both may not be ready for this. They may not even understand what the breakthrough means. In this Pulling It Together period you as the therapist often need to help them absorb what has happened. Sometimes you may need to give them some warnings about not moving too fast with next steps. You may want to instruct them to not do anything with the breakthrough—to just take the time to let it sink in. Or you may need to help them understand what has happened. Or you may need to answer some of their questions about what has happened and what it could mean.

There can be negative breakthroughs that require some damage control during this period. For example, in a current session Joyce and Ruth are working on why they have not been sexual for months. Joyce realizes that she has been angry for some time about how Ruth treats Joyce's family. As a result Joyce has withdrawn emotionally and sexually. Both women become quite upset at this realization. Ruth becomes teary and resentful at the same time. Joyce becomes defensive. In the last part of the session you as the therapist need to help them integrate this realization and give them some direction for handling these feelings after they have left the session. The couple is vulnerable to having a tense week after this session. How common it is that couples come in to the next session reporting that they had an argument after the last session! You can help ward this off by acknowledging this possibility and giving the couple guidelines for handling what has come up.

Therapist's Insights and Summary: Aha point 2

Sometimes the aha is that you provide an insight or summary of the work that the couple has done in order for them to more fully absorb what they have learned or discovered. Epstein and Baucom (1998) recount a therapist pulling together the learnings of a session:

> I think the two of you have come up with some good ideas that allow each person to carry our his or her positive intentions and also meet the needs of the other person. You are taking into account the fact that one's positive intentions aren't always carried out in the most effective manner, and that communicating with each other can clarify intentions and produce ways of carrying them out that are satisfying to both of you.
>
> (p. 57)

Directions for Dealing with the Issue: Ahas points 7a, 7d, and 7e

How do you help a couple find some direction for the work they have done? You might ask them how they are feeling toward each other, what they need from each other, what they have come to understand better about the other, and what they appreciate about the other through the work. You could ask the partners to sit opposite each other, make eye contact, and tell the other something they better understand about the other's needs. This is an example of point 7a. If the partners are unable to respond well to these inquiries or directions, it may be helpful for you as the therapist to say to them what you have seen during the sessions. For example, you might help one partner to see how the other has expressed caring during the work. You might reference an interaction that showed one partner dropping his/her defenses and opening up to the other. By using a soft tone yourself you could help the partners to soften toward each other.

Point 7d involves the couple connecting to external resources to help them with their issues. As an example, perhaps the couple has been arguing over finances during the session. Each thinks his/her way of handling their money is the right way. Through the session they have come to better understand each other's concerns. Now they need to have some help working out specific financial decisions. The last 10 minutes might be spent discussing the idea of going to a financial planner. If both are willing to do this, they could then discuss where to find some planners. It is usually helpful with this kind of issue for each person to agree to specific steps he/she is going to take before the next session.

Point 7e involves the couple making a plan to deal with their issues. Hoyt and Berg (1998) give dialogue from a case in which the wife is most unhappy about the husband's lack of participation with their children and with her. As the session draws to a close the wife expresses her desire to have close time together as they used to have. The wife agrees not to pressure the husband and the husband agrees to try his best to make time to be together.

17
Further Issues to Consider During Pulling It Together

What else might need attention during the Pulling It Together time period? As the therapist you might provide support for the couple. The couple may feel vulnerable, raw, and/or frustrated. At this point it may be very helpful for you to show empathy for what each partner is experiencing. During the session you may be confronting, directing traffic, changing the direction, or stopping an interaction. As the end of the session approaches, you may need to shift into a supportive mode in order to retain connection with the couple and help them integrate their work.

This period may be an important time to come back to something that was left behind during the session. Perhaps you saw an important interaction that was left hanging, needs reinforcement, and/or caused some feelings along the way. The session may have focused on other aspects of the issues. It may have gone in a different direction than where it started. There could be loose ends or something valuable that could be missed. This is the time to circle back to such concerns. One of the partners may have some concerns that he/she wants to raise before the session is done. Seeing that the session is coming toward an end, that partner may raise his/her concern. Or you as the therapist may need to raise it for him/her.

How such issues are raised is important, given the limits of time. The idea here is not to open a new chapter. Thus, you need to decide whether it is helpful for the issue to be discussed. If it is too involved, too emotional, too off-point, or too provocative, it is better not to return to it. It may be better to let it go and possibly raise it in the next session. If a partner raises an issue which is not helpful to explore, you may need to acknowledge the concern, talk about the lack of time to adequately deal with it, discuss dealing with it next time, or help the couple to let it go for now.

It is appropriate to go back to the issue if:

1 Some discussion can help to tie up loose ends.
2 Addressing the concern brings some important insight.
3 One partner has been the focus of the session and addressing the concern brings the other partner more into the session.
4 An important interaction in the session will be lost if it is not addressed.
5 Addressing the concern gives positive reinforcement to either partner and/or the relationship.
6 Doing so helps the partners connect better to you as the therapist or to each other.

What if a brand new issue arises in the last 10 minutes? Sometimes it can be addressed briefly and effectively during this period of time. Perhaps the couple is going on vacation and wants some pointers on how to be able to enjoy each other. Perhaps they have family who is coming and they want to discuss how to handle a certain relative. These examples may or may not be too complex and emotional to bring up anew at this point. The therapist must determine if the issue is a minefield to be avoided. If the couple is on the same page about the issue, if the issue has been addressed effectively before, if something can be accomplished in a short time, if the issue was raised in the beginning and it was decided it could wait until toward the end, then it may be helpful to deal with the concern. Another critical determiner of whether to change gears is whether the work of the session has been adequately addressed and processed. Clearly if this is not the case, this is not the time to open up something new.

What if there are 12 minutes left and there is no clear path to bringing things together? Occasionally it is important to leave the pieces lying around. When the couple is quite closed-up, when the work is stuck, when the couple would benefit from the boat being rocked—these are examples of times when it can be helpful for you to not bring things together during this period. In fact, you may want to emphasize how the pieces are not in place, how the partners are at odds, how the issues are not resolved. You may even want to pull things apart more in order to shake things up. All couples therapists know the experience of asking a couple how their week was and hearing that it was fine and nothing much happened. It may be as if the last session and others before did not happen. It may be that the session in progress is getting nowhere, like past sessions. Or it may be that the session has delved into important issues, but typically the couple closes up and does no further work on the issues. Each session may be like starting over again. During the session you may have been pushing them outside of their comfort zone. You may want to leave them there to see if they address the unresolved issues on their own.

Sometimes during this Pulling It Together period it is helpful for the couple to step back from the session and evaluate how the therapy is going. This evaluation can provide an overview of their work, tying in the work they have just done. This can be particularly helpful when the session has seemed disconnected from other sessions, when the couple seems to be floundering, when the session may indicate the need for a change of direction, when the couple has not been very engaged in the session, or when the couple may be ready to cut back their therapy.

18
Case Vignettes and Example for Pulling It Together

Case Vignette: Evaluating the Therapy

Cecilia and June spend the bulk of their session discussing Cecilia's concerns about June slipping in her recovery from obsessive use of pornography. June is working in individual therapy and is in a therapy group for sexual addiction. She had been caught by Cecilia a month ago for the second time with all kinds of pornography on her computer. In addition, she had been online in chat rooms sharing exciting porn sites. Cecilia is deeply hurt. June is quite remorseful about her behavior. She understands that Cecilia is feeling betrayed. They have been working on their recovery as a couple for some months. As the session comes toward the end, Cecilia wants to evaluate the therapy and get some guidelines about how to go forward as a couple. She wants to see some light at the end of the dark tunnel of her distrust.

Case Vignette: Making a Plan

In their couples session up to this point Jamie and Viktor had been discussing their wish to make their sexual relationship more interesting and exciting. They felt that their sexual life had become boring and they were both avoiding being sexual. This led to Jamie feeling resentful and Viktor withdrawing. They had discussed these issues in some previous sessions. The current session is focused on what to do. The meat of the session involves each of them saying what they wish for. It turns out that they each want to experience the other leading the way sexually. Viktor wants to be swept away by Jamie. He wishes she would take charge and initiate sexual activities. Jamie would like Viktor to show that he wants her. She wishes he would come on to her assertively, showing his masculinity. However, each of them wants to be the one who gives the signal of interest first. *Then* they want the other to take charge. Jamie acknowledges that for both of them the receiver is really the one in charge because he/she gives the signal of being interested. Working this out takes various attempts to explain; attempts that become confused and testy. When they discover that they each would like the same thing, there is a moment of revelation, surprise, and excitement. The last step is to put a plan in place. This involves a time and place for their activities. This part can be a challenge with sexual activities. Couples often have trouble envisioning how their wishes can actually play out. There are about 10 minutes left to set out a plan. It will be tricky to get this done before the end of the session. You as the therapist ask each partner where he/she would like to play out their scenario. Both excitedly say they want their plan to start in a bar/restaurant. They begin to play off each other as to which bar/restaurant they each prefer. The flirting begins with raising of eyebrows, sensual looks. All three laugh. Then comes the question of whether they want to have it happen spontaneously or whether they would like specific dates. Both are clear that they have to have specific dates or it won't happen. They look at their calendars to see possible nights they could go out.

Exciting as Viktor and Jamie's plan is, it could also be intimidating and scary. Avoidance is a clear possibility. Often you need to address the possibility that the couple might not follow through even when they set a date. If this were to happen, you need to urge the partners to reflect on what is happening inside themselves if they do not act on their plan. This discovery may be more important than their doing the plan. In this sense there is no "failure" when a plan is put in place.

Example of Pulling It Together in a Particular Type of Session

Some types of sessions described in the Full Steam Ahead period may require particular steps during this Pulling It Together period. Although there are no set steps for each type of session, there are common and recurring steps that are important for therapists to anticipate and utilize in a given type of session. An example of one particular type of session is presented here to show the issues and steps that may need to be considered during the Pulling It Together period

In some couples sessions you may be more focused on one of the partners. This type of session (Focusing on One Partner) is described in Full Steam Ahead, Chapter 13. You might have pushed one of the partners more, giving that person strong feedback, boundaries, and guidelines. You might have role-played some suggested behaviors for that person. You might have spoken for that person softening his/her communication to the other partner. You may have worked with that person's dilemmas, exploring feelings and discussing trauma, looking at that partner's history and family of origin, working on his/her parenting, or addressing his/her sexual dysfunction. Thus, sometimes this work may be more directly supportive and sometimes it may be more confrontive. In any of these cases it would be important at this point in the session to check in with this partner about how he/she is coping with being the subject of the focus of the session. If the focus has been supportive, he/she may feel your caring and concern. He/she could also be uncomfortable with this support, being unused to it, worrying about how the other partner feels, or feeling concerned that he/she is more of the problem. It would be important for this partner to voice any reactions. If they are not voiced, they could be lost or undermine the work. If you have been more confrontive, he/she may feel picked on, resentful, or even appreciative and seen. If you suspect that this partner feels picked on, it may be important to say something like, "I know I have pushed you today. I wonder if you have felt picked on," or, "How are you doing with my focusing more on you today." Sometimes a partner will respond, "Just make sure [X] gets a turn next time." This check-in is important for maintaining the relationship with the partner. It also models openness and processing that could be helpful for the couple.

It is likewise important to check in with the partner who has not been the focus. That partner could feel any number of things, such as relieved, left out, nervous, protective, annoyed, etc. He/she may be relieved that some important issue has been brought out or that the focus was not on him/her. He/she could feel left out because the other partner got the attention today. He/she could feel nervous that there will be negative fallout from the partner; or could feel protective that you were picking on the other or were bringing up difficult issues for the other; or could feel annoyed that you were being unfair. Here too it is important for the partner to be able to voice his/her feelings to maintain the relationship with you.

When one partner has been more the focus of the session, it is important before the session is over for you as the therapist to bring the couple back together and to connect. The above processing is an important step in this process. Further, you need to tie the work back into the couple's issues and concerns since this is couples therapy. This may involve discussion (1) connecting the work in this session to prior work, (2) connecting the active partner's work to issues of the less active partner, and (3) connecting the active partner's work into the couple's dynamics. It may also involve some couple emotional contact, such as having the less active partner reach out to the more active partner before the couple leaves.

19
Obstacles During Pulling It Together

Sometimes, oftentimes, sessions do not unfold as neatly as the one illustrated above. There might be 10 minutes and the partners are sniping at each other with nasty comments. Or a new explosive issue emerges. Or the session has not yet found a direction. Or one partner is upset with you, the therapist. In each of these scenarios you might be scrambling, nervous that the session is a waste. Nothing has been accomplished. Or worse, things are falling apart. The couple is perhaps worse off than when they came in. The session is a disaster. The organized neat flow that you hope for happens infrequently enough that it is important to look at the types of difficulties that can disrupt the therapist "Pulling It Together" in this 35 to 45-minute period.

Crescendo

The events of the session may become like a snowball increasing in emotional volume steadily throughout the session. You would like the crescendo to happen with enough time to process what has happened and for the couple to come to a calmer place. However, the emotional momentum may be building so that your best efforts to contain it at this point do not work.

For example, through the session Miranda is gradually coming to the realization that Betsy, in describing how different they are, is perhaps suggesting that they end their relationship. With 10 minutes left of the session Miranda bursts out with this perception and a well of tears. Betsy unconvincingly denies this, adding to Miranda's upset.

Minuchin and Nichols (1998) recount a case in which as the session comes toward the end, the couple is not communicating and is on the verge of a fight. The couple is losing control.

Lashing Out

Sometimes it may seem that one or both of the partners realize that there is not much time left in the session. They better get said what they have to say: something has been held back, something has not had time to be brought up, or something has been building up. As you are beginning to wind down the session, one of the partners lashes out and throws out a hand grenade. It may seem either out of the blue or out of proportion. The partner is often taken aback. Suddenly there is bleeding on the table just as you are stitching up the patients.

Darius and Darren had been arguing about whether their 16-year-old daughter had an issue with alcohol. Darius believed their daughter was doing what many 16-year-olds do when experimenting with drinking. Darren disagreed strongly, saying that she drank more than Darius knew and was hiding it from the two of them. They had been putting a plan in place to determine their daughter's drinking level when, toward the end of the session, Darren bursts out saying that he thinks Darius is a negligent parent and can't be trusted. Darius is aghast and bursts out crying.

Minuchin and Nichols (1998) recount the latter part of a session in which Minuchin decides to have the couple talk directly to each other. Rather than having constructive dialogue, the couple starts escalating, blaming, and attacking each other.

Clog in the Works

As you are attempting to pull things together, things may go awry. Below are examples of different clogs than can appear.

1 Barreling on through
  One or both partners keep the issues going. Your efforts to wrap up are ignored or openly flouted. The partners are intent on continuing

as if there is another half-hour ahead. One may say, "I have one more thing I have to say."

2 Dissent
A partner may express frustration, upset, or displeasure about the session. At this point, he/she might say, "I don't like where this is going." Or, "Things are worse than before we came in." Or, "This session has been a waste."

3 Running out of time
Fifty minutes is a very short time to do couples therapy. It is not uncommon to run out of time. The couple is in the middle of an issue. Insights are just beginning to arise. Help! More time is needed. No one wants to stop.

4 No sense
The therapy work does not make sense to the couple because of differences in the cultural values either between the partners or between the partners and the therapist. Hopefully any such conflict has emerged and been dealt with earlier in the session. However, the couple or a partner may not speak up until now. It may be important for you to check with the couple if you sense that they are not in sync with what had happened in the session.

5 New information
As you are pulling the session together, something brand new emerges. You want to put your head in your hands and say to yourself, "Oh, no." The new information may change the whole picture, disrupt what has developed, and upset the partners. It may be a game changer. Sometimes the partner giving this new information has only just become aware of it and/or did not intend to raise it. Or this partner has been afraid to mention it.

Case Vignette

Julienne and Laurence spend the therapy session dealing with tough issues about making a financial plan. Laurence has resisted making such a plan, saying that it isn't necessary. Juliette is the more organized one and the one who pays the bills. During the session Laurence reluctantly goes along with making some guidelines together to resolve their financial issues and get them on a budget. In the last 10 minutes of the session Laurence admits that he has $15,000 of credit card debt that Juliette does not know about. Juliette is shocked and angry that Laurence has this debt and that he has gone through making a plan without bringing this up. You as their couples therapist then have to decide what to do with this new information. Is there any way to integrate it into the plan? Do you need to process why Laurence has not admitted to this debt? What role might Juliette play in this information not emerging? What damage control do you need to do before the session ends? What possible homework can you give the couple to deal with this issue?

Misjudgment by the Therapist

Any of these scenarios can happen on their own or may be the result of a misjudgment by you as the couples therapist. This is tricky, delicate work. All couples therapists, even experienced ones, make misjudgments. They can happen in a flash. You did not catch the amount of emotion building. You forgot how charged this issue was. You were focused on something else. You were overwhelmed. Hopefully you recognize your mistake and make quick adjustments.

Darren's outburst toward the end of the session as described above could be a misjudgment by you the therapist if (1) Darren has been showing increased frustration during the session despite the plan being developed, (2) Darren has a history of such outbursts, or (3) you do not take into account important information about the extent of the daughter's drinking.

Unproductive Session

The session has gone nowhere. The couple has spent time repeating themselves despite your efforts to move things along. One partner has been uncooperative, blocking any progress. The couple has opened up issues, but nothing has come of it. You have tried various strategies that have not worked. We have all had these sessions. Now there are 10 minutes left and you are scrambling. What can you pull together in this time when nothing is working?

Gene and Charisse have gone over their lack of intimacy. Each has raised issues about the lack of involvement, ideas, initiation by the other. You have asked what they each would like. You have made suggestions that you thought might work for both partners based on what they have said. You have explored their fears of intimacy. Nothing has taken. What do you do now with 10 minutes left?

You need some last-minute strategies, some emergency measures, and some session-saving strategies. Below are some options.

1. Tell the partners the insights you have gathered from the session.
2. Give the couple praise for the work they have done, describing specific ways they have contributed, shared, opened up.
3. Be upfront about the current dilemma. Name it. For example, "It seems we have not made much progress with this issue today."
4. Encourage the couple to express their frustrations with the session.
5. Provide a framework that normalizes what has happened. Explain how this situation can occur in couples therapy and why. Put this session in context.
6. Tell the couple, if appropriate, that you see hope and why—that you see meaning in what has happened and why.
7. Show how what has happened is actually helpful, even though the partners may not see it.

These strategies are aimed to help the couple to be able to reconnect to the work of the session, find meaning in the session, regain emotional composure, learn about boundaries, and/or set and accept limits. They show how much couples work requires quick responses, enormous patience, and the ability to hold the big picture as well as a focus on the moment. There can be an obstacle ahead at any turn during a couples therapy session.

The Therapist's Experiences

Now that the session is nearing its end, you might think the Pulling It Together period would be straightforward. Clearly this is not the case. This time period draws on your ability to make sense out of what has happened and to convey that to the couple. This needs to happen whether or not the session makes sense to you. Sometimes you may feel like you are grabbing ideas of out thin air—or out of much too heavy air. Sometimes you do not know what you are going to say until you are saying it. You have been through this many times. You can do it again. This part of the session can be quite frustrating, quite satisfying, or both. If the loose ends are not coming together, if the couple is not getting it, you may feel overwhelmed, lost, or annoyed. When you make it work, when the couple participates in drawing the session to a meaningful close, you may feel a wonderful sense of accomplishment and completion. Sometimes during this period you are beginning to let down as the ahas emerge and the work comes to a close. Other times you are working hard, trying to find a way to pull the session together into something meaningful. Sometimes you wish there was more time, sometimes the time seems right, and sometimes you cannot wait for the session to be over and the couple to be gone. You may need some recovery time before your next couple.

Summary of Pulling It Together

This is the time to make sense of the work that has taken place. This section looks at what needs to happen as you the therapist pull the session together. There are many different types of ahas that often emerge. There may be brand new issues that come up. There may be issues from earlier in the session that need addressing. Plus there are any number of obstacles that can occur during this time. The next period involves the Ending of the session.

Section VII
Ending: 45–50 Minutes

20
Wrapping Up

The session is just about over. What needs to be said? What needs to be repeated? What will help the couple get through to the next session? This is the last chance to solidify what has happened in the session. This is the time for closing remarks. This is the time for words of wisdom. During these last few minutes you as the couples therapist might say such words as:

"In summary . . ."
"I hope you'll take away . . . from the session today."
"This session has been . . ."

It is helpful for therapists to have a checklist in their minds as the session ends. "Have I sufficiently supported each person? Was there an important statement I forgot to make? Is there something that still needs acknowledgment? An analogy can be made to when a person is about to leave his/her house for the day. It is helpful to have a mental checklist of everything that is needed for the day and anything in the house that needs last-minute attention.

This may be a time for you to briefly reflect with the couple on what kind of session has happened: a Skills-building session, a Breakthrough session, etc. This helps the couple understand what has taken place. You may comment on what has been helpful and/or difficult in the session. These thoughts help round out the container that is the couples therapy session. They reinforce the boundaries of the work. Part of the reflection may be mentioning what happened in the session to be sure the couple remembers it and/or to reinforce the importance of it. Partners may have different memories of what was said. Repetition can help head off disagreements. Any of these comments must be brief, given that the session is ending. Fuller discussion belongs in the previous period.

Freedman and Combs (2015) describe the ending of a session in which the therapist, after expressing regret that there was not more time to explore the issues, takes the time to, "name what stood out from the conversation." This is an example of summarizing as a way of ending the session. In a later session in the same case, the therapist ends the session by noting memories for the couple to come back to in the next meeting. This case is particularly helpful because the writers show how sessions end; something that most written cases do not include.

The ending may be a time to do a brief double-check on how each partner is doing. For example, "Is there something you need before you go?" This may also be a time for you to express any last-minute concerns that you have. Freedman and Combs (2015) in another session in their above case describe an ending in which the therapist asks the couple if the conversation in the session was helpful. The couple replies that, indeed, it was because "it had put them back in touch with the importance of their connection" (p. 290).

The ending of the session could be a time to check to make sure there are no misunderstandings from the session. Particularly in working with a couple from another country or culture, it may be important to check to make sure that the couple is not leaving confused. Confusion can happen as a result of language issues or differences in values and beliefs.

The ending may be a time to give homework to the couple. Homework can be given at any point during the session, depending on what is happening. If the homework is involved and complex, this is not the time to give it, for it will open up new concerns and feelings. The type of homework given at the end is summary homework. It is an extension of the work that has been done. You might say, "I'd like you to continue to . . .," or "I'd like you to commit to a time to . . .," or "There is a book I would like to recommend about what we have explored today." It is usually helpful to add that you will check back in about this homework next week. Couples sometimes ask for homework themselves. They may be looking for something to extend the session into their week.

As the session enters its end, you need to again think about what may happen after the session. There may be an immediate effect: the couple continues discussing the issues, they continue arguing, or they go out crying together and hugging. They may stand outside or sit in their car continuing the therapy session. There may be a longer-term effect: they stay close, they do not talk for several days, or they do not sleep together for a night. You may want to give the couple some directions for after the session such as to not talk about the session or to send each other some kind text messages during the day. Schlanger (2011) instructs a couple after a difficult session.

> I am going to give you a "doctor's prescription" that you actually don't talk to each other until then (the next session). I don't want you to discuss what each of you said during the session here, mostly to avoid recriminations which could lead to further conflict.
>
> (p. 139)

The end of a session may also be a time to make a plan for the next session. A plan may provide continuity for the therapy and give the couple some time to prepare for the next session. One partner may have an agenda that he/she wants to make sure gets addressed. Freedman and Combs (2002) in a different case study describe the end of a session as follows: "For Victoria, the next step would be to connect more emotionally and have more intimacy" (p. 328).

Case Vignette

The session had been particularly challenging for David. Roland had brought up a number of issues he had with David—issues that exposed David's vulnerabilities. As the session came to a close and the men were getting ready to leave, David's anger spilled out. It was evident that the couple was in for a difficult post-therapy time despite your earlier efforts to help David express his feelings. What do you do in this situation? Before the couple leaves, you might acknowledge David's anger, provide some containment for his anger, and/or reassure David that these issues will be addressed in the next session. If this had happened in the previous

Pulling It Together period when there was more time, you could help David to process his anger with the goal of finding a way to bring it to closure for now. At the very end of the session with 5 minutes left to go, you would need to be more directive, guiding David to contain his anger, hold on to his anger until next time, or find an appropriate way to express it after the session so the couple can indeed leave. These kinds of endings are very challenging for you to manage.

When you are concerned about the post-session effects, you need to address them with the couple. You may need to strongly advise the couple to wait until the next session to return to the difficult/volatile issues. The couple may need some help getting through the next week. You may need to give them some suggested boundaries, ideas for interacting, ways of sharing, or containing their feelings. Couples therapy sessions generate energy. What happens to this energy after? Where does it go? Sometimes you may advise the partners to do some reflecting on their own. Sometimes you may need to give them warnings—warnings about the possible effects of the session, warnings about behaviors that could get them into trouble, warnings about potholes to avoid. You might also ask them what they need. Epstein and Baucom (2002) write:

> Whenever there has been a tense or conflictual discussion between the partners during a session, the therapist can spend time toward the end of the session asking the couple what they can do to prevent their feelings from erupting into negative interactions at home during the hours and days ahead.
>
> (p. 277)

Sometimes it may be helpful for you to provide the transition from the session back into the regular world. This transition could consist of something like bringing up a quick distracting subject, talking about what they are going to do after the session, using some humor. Or you might address the transition directly, suggesting ideas for making the transition. For example, you might say, "Take your time leaving. You may need to sit in your car for a few minutes and take some deep breaths. You might want to do something mundane like go to the grocery store together." You might also talk about the next couples therapy session and what they might address. This can provide grounding, a sense of continuity, and/or direction.

There may be scheduling to do and payments to be made at the end of the session. Time needs to be allowed for this, particularly if there are any concerns involved. Couples can take up extra time trying to sync their schedules with your schedule. There may be new issues that arise during scheduling. Suddenly one partner says he/she wants to wait two weeks when they have been coming every week. Suddenly one is going to be away for business and the other did not know. Or suddenly an issue about money arises. Payment methods need to be established early on so that this is not an issue. The amount and the payment method need to be clear. Who pays needs to be established. Yet, there can be unexpected issues that arise. What if the insurance has changed? What if no one brought the means to pay? What if one of them suddenly expresses concern about the cost of the therapy? The point here is that as long as the couple is still in the room, issues can arise.

Case Vignette

Wilma and Roosevelt are finishing their session. Wilma is writing the check. Roosevelt looks at his calendar. The sessions have been weekly. "Oh," Roosevelt says, "I am going to be away the next three Thursdays." Wilma looks startled. Now there are a number of issues on the table. Where is Roosevelt going to be? Why doesn't Wilma know about it? Why is this coming up now as the session is over? What will be the effect on the couple's therapy of a four-week unplanned hiatus? Can the sessions be rescheduled? All this with no time to deal with these issues. You may need to say something like, "Let's go ahead and schedule a session for when Roosevelt gets back. Then we will have a session on the books. In the meantime there are some important issues that have arisen in these last few minutes. I suggest you talk about them together using the skills we have been working on together." A response like this acknowledges what is happening and attempts to give some guidance to the couple for when they leave. Wilma and Roosevelt may become the couple sitting in their car after the session arguing.

The Therapist's Experience

You may be thinking, "Let's get this done." Or, "I still need more time." Or, "Please let there not be any more last-minute issues." Or, "Wow, this has been an amazing session." This may be the time when some of your own feelings about the work you have done bubble up. Can you finish the job? How has it gone? Your guard may start to come down. You may even be transitioning to the next session. Couples therapy training does not necessarily prepare you for how to end a session. The focus is on the body of the work. Yet you need to stay fully engaged. You need to watch for your own feelings and self-judgments.

Summary of Ending

Ending is time for the work to be finished and for the couple to go on their way. During this time you as the therapist mttay give a summary of the session, assign final homework, and/or help the couple with a transition back to their day. Payment and scheduling may be addressed. Challenging issues such as handling post-session effects may arise. The session is over, but not completely since the couple has yet to leave. The last section involves the couple going out the door.

Section VIII
Leaving

21
DEPARTING

Most of the time leavings are quick and simple. "Have a good week," "Have a good trip," "I hope the weather is better," "Thanks," are typical ending statements. As the therapist, you stand by the door as the couple goes out. Sometimes partners will use humor. "Whew! I'm glad the bell rang." "I'm glad I survived that." The humor may also communicate a message. Sometimes partners are looking for a last-minute something (reassurance, caring, etc.) from the therapist. For example one partner might say, "I'll bet you're glad that we are leaving."

Sometimes one or both of the partners is especially appreciative of you at the end of the session. Minuchin and Nichols (1998) tell of a wife saying to Minuchin as the couple leaves, "What would we do without you?" (p. 119). Minuchin simply smiles back at her.

Leaving may be a time to acknowledge a couple's cultural background: a goodbye in their language, a recognition of their upcoming religious holiday, i.e. something low-key and appropriate.

Sometimes partners want to engage the therapist personally at the end. For example, one might ask about where the therapist is going for vacation or one might express concern for the therapist's foot which is recuperating from surgery. The therapist needs to assess the intent of the partner in addressing the therapist on a personal level. Is this small talk? Does the partner really want to know the answer? Is this a way for the partners to provide a transition back out into their day? What will the partners do with any personal information? You as the therapist need to be clear about your policy with regard to personal disclosure and how to handle this situation. If there is an obvious health issue that you have, what do you say to inquiries and worries about your health? This kind of situation may be uncomfortable for you.

Couples therapists have all experienced awkward leavings. One partner is still upset. One storms out. The couples therapist needs to do his/her best to smooth out the leaving if it is not going well. The session is over, so the smoothing needs to be careful and not re-engaging. Sometimes one partner has left and the remaining partner is doing the scheduling and making the payment. What happens if the remaining partner begins to express feelings about the partner who has left or to ask questions of you as the therapist? You need to be cautious and neutral so as not to re-engage the partner. Or you may need to affirm that you cannot talk about these issues when the other partner is not there. If the remaining partner is distraught, you may want/need to help this partner to be able to leave. Some supportive words and some transitional suggestions are likely to be helpful.

Some couples are reluctant or nervous about leaving. Perhaps they fear being without a mediator for a week. Perhaps they like the safety of the therapy sessions. Perhaps they fear the after-effects of the session. Some couples may draw out the leaving. Most couples therapists have had the experience of almost having to shoo a couple out the door. Some partners will attempt to engage the therapist on issues related to the therapy and some will try to engage the therapist on unrelated issues, such as a national issue or the success of the regional sports team. It can be tempting to engage with the couple if the subject is of interest to the therapist. (Will the local team win the World Series this year?) It may be fine for the therapist to engage for a minute or two at the door. Longer than a few minutes tends to extend the therapy session, even if the topic is not about therapy.

Some couples cannot wait to leave. They may go out abruptly and barely say goodbye. Abrupt leavings may indicate that the couple does not know how to handle the transition between therapy and their lives. Or they may not know how to relate to you as the therapist outside of the session, so they make it brief. Abrupt leavings might be important to bring up during the session at some point if they reflect an issue about the therapy or one within the couple.

Therapists know the expression, "doorknob therapy." This refers to the clients bringing up a loaded issue right as they are leaving. It can also refer to attempts by clients to get some more therapy even as they leave. When this happens with a couple, the situation can be particularly difficult because it may mean the couple will be leaving with issues hanging open. You need to close down doorknob therapy attempts quickly, hopefully before they get one or the other partner charged up. You might say something like, "Let's address this next time," or "We don't have time left to address this, so I think it would be better to put it away for now." Not only is it important to stop the process, but it is also important to attend to doing so in a clear and thoughtful way so that the couple does not leave feeling upset with you. This can be delicate.

The issues in this Leaving section illustrate how, until the couple is out of sight, each moment of the session can be significant. You need to be conscious and attentive every minute. It is part of what makes this work exciting and challenging.

If business dealings such as handing you a check and affirming a regular schedule are routine, they may happen during the Leaving period. (They are more likely to have happened in the Ending period.) This more mundane and concrete interacting can provide a helpful transition for the couple back into their day-to-day world. It can help them to let go of the sometimes intense and difficult issues they have explored in the session. Thus, these transactions can be grounding. However, if issues arise about payment and scheduling, they cannot be dealt with at this point. You would need to make a quick decision as to what to do. Most likely you would need to say that they need to call you about the issue or wait until the next session to address it.

The Therapist's Experiences

The therapy is over and the couple is leaving. Were we ever trained to deal with all these possible last-minute issues? Probably not. We may have let our guard down and now find ourselves getting caught in a jam. Using the trip analogy, we have arrived at our destination. We are done, right? Not exactly. We are still in the car. We could trip getting out of the door. The car may not be in park and the motor won't turn off. We need to be conscious of where we put the keys. Handling the leaving most of the time is simple enough. Then there are those other times, as explored above. These times can test our boundaries. They can test our energy if there is yet more required of us. We may feel like a wet dishrag. We may feel annoyed or challenged. Hopefully we feel satisfied with the session and ready for any last-minutes needs as the couple exits.

Case Vignette

As Marliana and Carolina are about to leave their couples therapy session, Marliana turns to you the therapist and says, "Can I give you a hug?" As she says this, you notice that Carolina is glaring at Marliana. Marliana sees you look toward Carolina and quickly says, "Oh, Carolina doesn't like hugs." You, who do not give clients hugs, do not want to reject Marliana. You also see that Carolina is annoyed and that there are some couple issues embedded in this interaction. You say to the couple, "This is something that would be good to talk about when we have the time. Let's wait for now and bring this up later." Marliana then says, "Well, it's no big deal." Carolina meanwhile has gone outside into the hall. You then simply say, "Let's hold on this for now. See you both next week." There are layers of issues to discuss in this interaction and there is no time to deal with anything more.

Summary of Leaving

Leaving seems easy enough. Yet, there are still issues that can arise. Are there last-minute issues that crop up? How does the couple feel about leaving? What if a partner asks you something personal as the couple departs? There are different types of leavings, such as reluctant leavings, abrupt leavings, and awkward leavings. A session is not completely over until the couple has gone.

Section IX
Summary Case Study

22
Case Study

This section presents a case study illustrating a session from beginning to end. Each of the time frames discussed in this book is presented through the case.

Background Information

Cheryl and Ian had been struggling with issues about Cheryl's relationships with other men. Ian described Cheryl as flirting inappropriately with a male neighbor. He also described her relationship with a certain man at work as being inappropriate. He said that she spent coffee hours with this male coworker, that she drove this man to different work sites, and that she texted with this man often. Cheryl, however, did not see a problem with her relationship with this man or with the neighbor. She described herself as being a friendly and open person and that she was not going to change. She agreed that some of her behaviors were hurtful to Ian and that she would keep some boundaries with the man at work. Ian was glad for these boundaries, but he wanted to hear Cheryl admit that her behavior had been inappropriate. Furthermore, he wanted Cheryl to tell him why she had acted in these ways. He tended to grill Cheryl with questions, attempting to analyze her behavior. When they discussed these issues, it went nowhere. In the therapy sessions they got into vehement "he-said-she-said" blaming interactions with Ian trying to drive home his points and with Cheryl rolling her eyes as she described him as overreacting.

With guidance from you their couples therapist, they had decided to work on other less charged issues to build their communication skills. On issues that were much less charged, they had made progress in owning their own viewpoints, sharing their feelings, and seeing their contributions to their disputes. They were getting impatient to get to the issue of other men.

The Session

Cheryl and Ian come into the current session at 2pm laughing and talking about buying stones for a new walkway they are putting in. You decide to extend the lightheartedness and positive feelings by engaging the couple about their walkway for a few minutes. This sets a tone of easy engagement. Then you ask how they are doing thinking that they would report a positive week.

Both Cheryl and Ian report that they had had a good week in which they felt close. In addition, they report some interactions with Cheryl's mother. Both of their relationships with her mother are strained, but they are on the same page about the issues involved. They had discussed this in a recent past session. That discussion had led to some agreed-upon actions to take in dealing with Cheryl's mother. The conversation shifts to Cheryl's ex-husband. They are in agreement about how difficult he is. He often hassles Cheryl about money, attempting to find ways to limit his alimony.

Tension begins to arise in this session about some past incidents in which Ian believes that Cheryl had spent too much time talking with her ex-husband. Ian maintains that Cheryl ignored him. His voice is rising and his tone is becoming sharp. Cheryl downplays these incidents waving them off. You stop them to ask if talking about this would be as difficult as dealing with the issues about other men. You are concerned that this issue might be too charged. In addition, you ask if they think they can use the skills that they have been practicing to have a productive conversation about these incidents. They both agree that they think that they can talk about this issue productively despite the rising tension. You are a bit wary, being concerned that the session could easily veer off into their rancorous patterns. You go on high alert ready for their verbal attacks on each other. Will they fall into old patterns? You are caught between their impatience to deal with the issue of men and your doubts about how this is going. You decide that it would be best if the session shows them whether they are ready to deal with this issue. You also think they might be able to rein it in and work productively. At this point the session is 15 minutes into the 50-minute session. It is 2:15. There is a plan. It is time to dig into the work!

As they start, you review in your mind how talking about an ex-spouse can be tricky. You ask Cheryl and Ian to give some background to the incidents about Cheryl's ex-husband. You do this to get the information and to defuse the tension that had started to develop. Ian describes that Cheryl text-messages her ex-husband and talks with him by phone often. Cheryl denies this saying that she communicates with her ex only occasionally and only about the children. Ian says that since their children are grown, Cheryl does not need to be communicating with her ex about them. You talk with them about the difference in their viewpoints of the situation. You make an attempt to have them each own their own perspective on the situation. Neither of them is willing to do this. In fact, Ian begins to get angry that Cheryl will not admit how often she communicates with her ex-husband. Again you intervene and ask each of them to step back for a minute and use the skills that they have been practicing in prior sessions. Cheryl responds by defending her behavior and claiming her innocence. You intervene to try to slow down the interaction between them. You ask for more information about the situation. Cheryl then explains that two of her three adult children are dealing with health issues and she has recently been more in touch with her ex-husband. This possibly explains Ian's perception about the frequency of Cheryl's communication with her ex. Ian, however, does not accept that there is an increase in the communication only lately. He shoots back with saying that her children have had health issues for some time. Soon they are into their old pattern of blaming each other. You stop the interactions and ask them to take some deep breaths. You ask them to recognize that they are into their old patterns. Both acknowledge that this is true. However, both are quite flooded. Ian's face is red. Cheryl is tight-mouthed and she sits rigidly in her chair. You are on edge yourself. The session is going off the rails. The goodwill they have built up over the last weeks is going out the window.

It is now 2:35. Only 15 minutes to go. How will you pull this session out? Should you go further with pointing out their old patterns? Should you ask each one to stop and talk about his/her own feelings. Should you ask each to make "I" statements? Should you ask them to sit quietly to de-flood first? Perhaps then they will realize they have lost it. This intervention is often helpful to them when they become flooded. One idea after another races through your mind while Cheryl and Ian are escalating. You realize something needs to happen quickly or the session will be a disaster and previous work will seem to have evaporated.

Then you hear yourself talking . . . telling Ian and Cheryl what you are going to do. You tell them that you are going to speak for each one of them saying the feelings and concerns that you think underlie each of their positions right then. You start with Cheryl because you know that she needs support the most. She often feels drowned out by Ian's more strident insistent voice. She is often the one who is "wrong" and he the aggrieved one.

You speak as Cheryl. "I feel misunderstood. I don't mean to hurt anyone. In these situations I don't know how to get it right. I feel judged by you as if I am scum. I want to be pleasant to my ex-husband for my children's sake. Do you think I want to talk with my ex-husband? You know I dread talking to him. Not just because of how you feel. I myself . . ." You go on. Cheryl is nodding in agreement. Her face becomes more relaxed. The flush on her face abates some.

Then you turn to Ian. "I feel left out when you talk with your ex. Sometimes I imagine that you want to be back with him even though I know you don't. You have such a bond together over your children. You go through things together that are very emotional and heart-wrenching. I hear how much you share together and I feel alone in the other room." Ian has tears rolling down his checks. His head is bent down. At this point Cheryl is looking over at him with caring. She is still guarded, but some of the ice has broken.

In sessions such as this when you speak for partners, you prefer that each partner then put into his/her own words what you have said because this helps the partners to own the work. What emerges might be similar or different than what you have said. In this session there is not time for Cheryl and Ian to speak for themselves. Also, they are not ready to do so in a constructive way. Leaving them in the atmosphere of your careful words of empathy and understanding is helping them to bridge their divide.

You ask each of them how it is to hear you speak for him/her. Ian says that you have expressed just what he is feeling. Cheryl says thank you. She murmurs that it feels so good to be understood. It is 2:45. How will you wrap this up and send them on?

You talk about the depth of feelings in each of them. You speak about how hard it is for each of them to express his/her deeper feelings. You say you hope that by your surfacing these feelings they can feel understood and better understand each other. You tell them that they might not be able to reach out to each other at this point and that that is OK, given how wounded each feels. You guide them to take time to absorb the feelings and experiences that you have expressed for them. As Cheryl and Ian finish the session in silence and Ian writes the check, you wonder if they can hold onto the apparent softening that has happened between them. As they stand up and get ready to head for the door, Cheryl reaches out to Ian and puts her arm around his waist. He becomes more teary as he moves closer to her and they walk out of the door. As they go out into the waiting room, you feel a bit teary yourself.

Reflections on the Session

The Lead-in to this session was pleasant and lighthearted. You extended this goodwill into the Beginning of the session. You then began with an open-ended approach to see how the couple was doing. This led to the issue of Cheryl's interactions with her ex-husband. Due to the tension between Cheryl and Ian, Cheryl's contact with her ex-husband became the direction of the session (Finding a Direction). However, Establishing the Work was difficult. You attempted to slow the session down by asking for background about the issues. You negotiated with the couple about whether they could have a productive discussion. You tried to help the couple to see each other's point of view. Nothing was working. The session was becoming a Session Gone Wrong. By now the session needed to be in Full Steam Ahead, but it was not. Then you instinctively shifted to speaking for the partners. You expressed the underlying feelings that you were picking up from each partner. This helped to calm the session. Each of the partners felt heard. In the Pulling It Together period you then processed how each partner felt, listening to you. The session had become a Turnaround session through you using the technique of speaking for the partners. In the Ending you summarized the session and shared your hopes as to how the session might help the partners. You gave them some guidelines for after the session. The couple came together in a touching way during their Leaving.

BIBLIOGRAPHY

Addison, S.M. & Thomas, V. (2010). Searching for mutuality: A feminist/multicultural approach to couple therapy. In A.S. Gurman (Ed.), *Clinical casebook of couple therapy,* (pp. 281–307). New York: Guilford Press.

Anger-Diaz, B. & Anger, K. (2011). Mental research institute's brief therapy approach to couple therapy. In D.K. Carson & M. Casado-Kehoe (Eds.), *Case studies in couples therapy* (pp. 145–160). New York: Routledge.

Apfelbaum, B. (1995). Masters and Johnson revisited: A case of desire disparity. In. R.C. Rosen & S.R. Lieblum (Eds.), *Case studies in sex therapy* (pp. 23–45). New York: Guilford Press.

Appell, J. (2006). *Divorce doesn't have to be that way: A handbook for the helping professional.* Atascadero, CA: Impact Publishers.

Atkinson, B.J. (2010). Rewiring emotional habits: The pragmatic/experiential method. In A.S. Gurman (Ed.), *Clinical casebook of couple therapy* (pp. 181–207). New York: Guilford Press.

Bader, E. & Pearson, P.T. (2000). *Tell me no lies: How to face the truth and build a loving marriage.* New York: St. Martin's Press.

Bagnini, C. (2011). Object-relations therapy with couples. In D.K. Carson & M. Casado-Kehoe (Eds.), *Case studies in couples therapy* (pp. 65–78). New York: Routledge.

Baucom, D.H., Epstein, N.B., Kirby, J.S. & LaTaillade, J.J. (2015). Cognitve-behavioral couple therapy. In A.S. Gurman, J.L. Lebow & D.K. Snyder (Eds.), *The clinical handbook of couples therapy* (5th ed., pp. 23–60). New York: Guilford Press.

Baucom, D.H., Epstein, N. & LaTaillade, J.L. (2002). Cognitive-behavioral couple therapy. In A.S. Gurman & N.S. Jacobson, N. (Eds.), *The clinical handbook of couple therapy* (3rd ed., pp. 26–58). New York: Guilford Press.

Birchler, G.R., Fals-Stewart, W. & O'Farrell, T.J. (2005). Couples therapy for alcoholism and drug abuse. In J.L. Lebow (Ed.), *Handbook of clinical family therapy* (pp. 251–180). Hoboken, NJ: John Wiley & Sons.

Bok, S. (1982). *Secrets.* New York: Pantheon Books.

Boyd-Franklin, N., Kelly, S. & Durham, J. (2008). African American couples in therapy. In A.S. Gurman (Ed.), *The clinical handbook of couples therapy* (4th ed., pp. 681–693). New York: Guilford Press.

Brazier, D.D. (1993). Key concepts of phenomenological therapy. Retrieved October 2, 2008 from www.amidatrust.com/article_phen.html.

Brok, A. (2011). Working with couples from a psychodynamic perspective using cognitive maps. In D.K. Carson & M. Casado-Kehoe (Eds.), *Case studies in couples therapy* (pp. 53–64). New York: Routledge.

Carson, D.K. & Casado-Kehoe, M. (2011). Creative/experiential therapy with couples. In D.K. Carson & M. Casado-Kehoe (Eds.), *Case studies in couples therapy* (pp. 229–248). New York: Routledge.

Christensen, A.C., Wheeler, J.G. & Jacobson, N.S. (2008). Couple distress. In. D.H. Barlow (Ed.), *Clinical handbook of psychological disorders* (4th ed., pp. 662–689). New York: Guilford Press.

Christensen, A., Dimidjian, S. & Martell, C.S. (2015). Integrative Behavioral Couple Therapy. In A.S. Gurman, J.L. Lebow & D.K. Snyder (Eds.), *The clinical handbook of couples therapy* (5th ed., pp. 61–94). New York: Guilford Press.

Dickerson, V.C. & Crockett, K. (2010). El tigre, el tigre: A story of narrative practice. In A.S. Gurman (Ed.), *Clinical casebook of couple therapy* (pp. 153–180). New York: Guilford Press.

Dickson, J. Dattilio, F.M. & Cherrington, L. (2011). Cogntive behavior therapy with couples. In D.K. Carson & M. Casado-Kehoe (Eds.), *Case studies in couples therapy* (pp. 93–107). New York: Routledge.

Dworkian, S.H. & Pope, M. (2012). *Casebook for counseling: Lesbian, gay, bisexual and transgendered persons and their families*. Alexandria, VA: America Counseling Association.

Emery, R.E. & Sbarra, D.A. (2002). Separation and divorce. In A.S. Gurman & N. Jacobson (Eds.), *The clinical handbook of couples therapy* (3rd ed., pp. 508–530). New York: Guilford Press.

Epstein, N.B. & Baucom, D.H. (1998). Cognitive-behavioral couple therapy. In F.M. Dattilio (Ed.), *Case studies in couple and family therapy* (pp. 37–61). New York: Guilford Press.

Epstein, N.B. & Baucom, D.H. (2002). Conducting couples therapy. In N.B. Epstein & D.H. Baucom (Eds.), *Enhanced cognitive-behavioral therapy for couples: A contextual approach* (pp. 269–293). Washington, DC: American Psychological Association.

Feutz, C. (2004). The emotionally distant couple: Creating new bridges. In J. Schwartz Gottman (Ed.), *The marriage clinic: Casebook* (pp. 109–129). New York: W.W. Norton & Company.

Fishbane (2010). Relational empowerment in couple therapy: An integrative approach. In A.S. Gurman (Ed.), *Clinical casebook of couple therapy* (pp. 181–207). New York: Guilford Press.

Freedman, J.H. & Combs, G. (2002). Narrative couple therapy. In A.S. Gurman & N. Jacobson (Eds.), *The clinical handbook of couples therapy* (3rd ed., pp. 322–334). New York: Guilford Press.

Freedman, J. & Combs, G. (2015). Narrative couple therapy. In A.S. Gurman, J.L. Lebow & D.K. Snyder (Eds.), *The clinical handbook of couples therapy* (5th ed., pp. 271–299). New York: Guilford Press.

Germer, C.K. & Siegel, R.D. (Eds.) (2013). *Mindulness and psychotherapy* (2nd ed.). New York: Guilford Press.

Glass, S.P. (2002). Infidelity. In A.S. Gurman & N. Jacobson (Eds.), *The clinical handbook of couples therapy* (3rd ed., pp. 488–507). New York: Guilford Press.

Goldman, R.N. & Greenberg, L.S. (2010). Self-soothing and other-soothing in emotion-focused therapy for couples. In A.S. Gurman (Ed.), *Clinical casebook of couple therapy* (pp. 255–280). New York: Guilford Press

Gollan, J.K., Friedman, M.A. & Miller, I. W. (2002). Couple therapy in the treatment of major depression. In A.S. Gurman & N. S. Jacobson (Eds.), *The clinical handbook of couple therapy* (3rd ed., pp. 653–676). New York: Guilford Press.

Gottman, J. (1999). *The seven principles for making marriage work*. New York: The Three Rivers Press.

Green, R.J. & Mitchell, V. (2015). Gay, lesbian and bisexual issues in couple therapy. In A.S. Gurman, J.L. Lebow & D.K. Snyder (Eds.), *The clinical handbook of couples therapy* (5th ed., pp. 489–511). New York: Guilford Press.

Greenan, D.E. (2010). Therapy with a gay male couple. In A.S. Gurman (Ed.), *Clinical casebook of couple therapy* (pp. 102–111). New York: Guilford Press.

Greenan, D.E. & Tunnell, G. (2003). *Couple therapy with gay men.* New York: Guilford Press.

Gurman, A.S. (Ed.) (2010). *Clinical casebook of couple therapy.* New York: The Guilford Press.

Hall, K.S.K. & Graham, C.A. (2014). Culturally sensitive sex therapy: The need for shared meanings in the treatment of sexual problems. In Y.M. Binik & K.S.K. Hall (Eds.), *Principles and practice of Sex Therapy* (5th ed., pp. 334–358). New York: Guilford Press.

Hamburg, S.R. (2010). Getting over a rough spot: A short-term, problem-focused approach. In A.S. Gurman (Ed.), *Clinical casebook of couple therapy* (pp. 308–330). New York: Guilford Press.

Hanna, F.J. (2005). *Therapy with difficult clients: Using the precursors method to awaken change.* Washington, DC: American Psychological Association.

Hardy, K.V. & Laszloffy, T.A. (2002). Couple therapy using a multicultural perspective. In A.S. Gurman & N. Jacobson (Eds.), *The clinical handbook of couples therapy* (3rd ed., pp. 569–593). Guilford Press: New York.

Hazlett, P.S. (2010). Attunement, disruption, and repair: The dance of self and other in emotionally focused couple therapy. In A.S. Gurman (Ed.), *Clinical casebook of couple therapy* (pp. 21–43). New York: Guilford Press.

Hertlein, K.M., Weeks, G.R. & Sendak, S.K. (2009). *A clinician's guide to systemic sex therapy* (pp. 32–44). New York: Routledge.

Hoyt, M.F. (2015). Solution-focused couple therapy. In A.S. Gurman, J.L. Lebow & D.K. Snyder (Eds.), *The clinical handbook of couples therapy* (5th ed., pp. 300–322). New York: Guilford Press.

Hoyt, M.F. & Berg, I.K. (1998). Solution-focused couple therapy: Helping clients construct self-fulfilling realities. In F.M. Dattilio (Ed.), *Case studies in couple and family therapy* (pp. 203–232). New York: Guilford Press.

Imber-Black, E. (1993). Secrets in families and family therapy: An overview. In E. Imber-Black (Ed.), *Secrets in families and family therapy* (pp. 3–28). New York: W.W. Norton.

Johnson, S.M. (2015). Emotionally focused couple therapy. In A.S. Gurman, J.L. Lebow & D.K. Snyder (Eds.), *The clinical handbook of couples therapy* (5th ed., pp. 97–128). New York: Guilford Press.

Karpel, M.A. (1994). *Evaluating couples.* New York: W.W. Norton & Co.

Kayser, K. & Rao, S.S. (2006). Process of disaffection in relationship breakdown. In M.A. Fine & J.H. Harvey (Eds.), *Handbook of divorce and relationship dissolution* (pp. 201–221). Mahwah, NJ: Lawrence Erlbaum Associates.

Keim, J. & Lappin, J. (2008). Structural-strategic couple therapy. In A.S. Gurman & N. Jacobson (Eds.), *The clinical handbook of couples therapy* (3rd ed., pp. 86–117). New York: Guilford Press.

Kelly, A. (2002). *The psychology of secrets.* New York: Kluwer Academic/Plenum.

Killian, K.D. (2015). Couple therapy and intercultural relationships. In A.S. Gurman, J.L. Lebow & D.K. Snyder (Eds.), *The clinical handbook of couples therapy* (5th ed., pp. 512–528). New York: Guilford Press.

Korelitz, A.Z. (1982). Dealing with sexual secrets in conjoint therapy. In A.S. Gurman (Ed.), *Questions and answers in the practice of family therapy*, vol. 2 (pp. 105–107). New York: Bruner/Mazel.

Leavitt, J. (2009). *Common dilemmas in couple therapy.* New York: Routledge.

Llerene-Quinn, R. & Bacigalupe, G. (2009). Constructions of difference among Latino/Latina immigrant and non-Hispanic white couples. In T.A. Karis & K.D. Killian (Eds.), *Intercultural couples: Exploring diversity in intimate relationships* (pp. 167–187). New York: Routledge.

Maltz, W. (2012). *The sexual healing journey: A guide for survivors of sexual abuse* (3rd. ed.). New York: HarperCollins Publishers.

Maltz, L. & Maltz, W. (2010). *The porn trap: The essential guide to overcoming problems caused by pornography.* Novato, CA: New World Library.

McCarthy, B.W. (2002). Sexuality, sexual dysfunction and couple therapy. In A.S. Gurman & N. Jacobson (Eds.), *The clinical handbook of couples therapy* (3rd ed., pp. 629–652). New York: Guilford Press.

McCarthy, B.W. & Bodnar, L.E. (2005). Couple sex therapy: Assessment, treatment and relapse prevention. In J.L. Lebow (Ed.), *Handbook of clinical family therapy* (pp. 464–493). Hoboken, NJ: John Wiley & Sons.

McCarthy, B.W. & Thestrup, M. (2008). Couple therapy and the treatment of sexual dysfunction. In A.S. Gurman (Ed.), *The clinical handbook of couples therapy* (4th ed., pp. 591–617). New York: Guilford Press.

McLendon, J.A. & Robert Bitter, J. (2011). A path to wholeness: Couple therapy with the Satir model. In D.K. Carson and M. Casado-Kehoe (Eds.), *Case studies in couples therapy* (pp. 177–190). New York: Routledge.

Minuchin, S. & Nichols, M.P. (1998). Structural family therapy. In F.M. Dattilio (Ed.), *Case studies in couple and family therapy* (pp. 108–131). New York: Guilford Press.

Perls, F. (1969). *Gestalt therapy verbatim.* Lafayette, CA: Real People Press.

Perls, F. (1973). *The Gestalt Approach and Eye Witness to Therapy.* Ben Lomond, CA: Science and Behavioral Books.

Pierce, W.J. & Elisme, E. (1991). Understanding and working with Haitian immigrant families. In P.M. Brown & J.S. Shalett (Eds.), *Cross-cultural practice with couples and families* (pp. 40–66). New York: The Haworth Press.

Rohrbaugh, M.J. & Shoham, V. (2015). In A.S. Gurman, J.L. Lebow & D.K. Snyder (Eds.), *The clinical handbook of couples therapy* (5th ed., pp. 335–357). New York: Guilford Press.

Rollie, S.S. & Duck, S. (2006). Divorce and dissolution of romantic relationships: Stage models and their limitations. In M.A. Fine & J.H. Harvey (Eds.), *Handbook of divorce and relationship dissolution* (pp. 221–240). Mahwah, NJ: Lawrence Erlbaum Associates.

Rosen, R.C. (1995). A case of premature ejaculation: Too little, too late? In. R.C. Rosen & S.R. Lieblum (Eds.), *Case studies in sex therapy* (pp. 279–294). New York: Guilford Press.

Rosen, R.C. & Lieblum, S.R. (Eds.) (1995). *Case studies in sex therapy.* New York: Guilford Press.

Ruddy, N.B. & McDaniel, S.H. (2002). Couple therapy and medical issues: Working with couples facing medical illness. In A.S. Gurman & N. Jacobson (Eds.), *The clinical handbook of couples therapy* (3rd ed., pp. 699–716). New York: Guilford Press.

Sawyer, M. (2004). Bridging psychodynamic couples therapy and Gottman method couples therapy. In J. Schwartz Gottman (Ed.), *The marriage clinic casebook* (pp. 181–196). New York: W.W. Norton & Company.

Scharff, J.S. & Bagnini, C. (2002). Object relations couple therapy. In A.S. Gurman & N. Jacobson (Eds.), *The clinical handbook of couples therapy* (3rd ed., pp. 59–85). New York: Guilford Press.

Schlanger, K. (2011). Problem-solving brief therapy: The Palto Alto approach to working with a Latino couple. In D.K. Carson & M. Casado-Kehoe (Eds.), *Case studies in couples therapy* (pp. 133–144). New York: Routledge.

Schnarch. D. (1991). *Constructing the sexual crucible.* New York: W.W. Norton & Company.

Schwartz Gottman, J. (2004). Extramarital affairs: The pearl in the oyster. In J. Schwartz Gottman (Ed.), *The marriage clinic casebook* (pp. 46–68). New York: W.W. Norton & Company.

Schwartz Gottman, J. (Ed.) (2004). *The marriage clinic casebook.* New York: W.W. Norton & Company.

Shapiro, J.L. (2010). At the risk of losing our misery: Existential couple therapy. In A.S. Gurman (Ed.), *Clinical casebook of couple therapy* (pp. 398–426). New York: Guilford Press.

Simon, G.M. (2015). Structural couple therapy. In A.S. Gurman, J.L. Lebow & D.K. Snyder (Eds.), *The clinical handbook of couples therapy* (5th ed., pp. 358–384). New York: Guilford Press.

Slavik, S., Carlson, J. & Sperry, L. (1998). The passive-aggressive couple. In J. Carlson & L. Sperry (Eds.), *The disordered couple* (pp. 299–314). Bristol, PA: Brunner/Mazel.

Snyder, D.K., Schneider, W.J. & Castellani, A.M. (2003). Tailoring couple therapy to individual differences: A conceptual approach. In D.K. Snyder & M.A. Whisman (Eds.), *Treating difficult couples* (pp. 27–51). New York: Guilford Press.

Soloman, M.F. (2010). The me nobody knows: Attachment repair in couple therapy. In A.S. Gurman (Ed.), *Clinical casebook of couple therapy* (pp. 355–374). New York: Guilford Press.

Spinelli, E. (1989). *The interpreted world: An introduction to phenomenological psychology.* London: Sage Publications.

Spring, J.A. (1997). *After the affair: Healing the pain and rebuilding trust when a partner has been unfaithful.* New York: HarperCollins Publishers.

Stendhal, R. (2003). *True secrets of lesbian desire.* Berkeley, CA: North Atlantic Books.

Weeks, G.R., Odell, M. & Methven, S. (2005). *If only I had known: Avoiding common mistakes in couples therapy.* New York: W.W. Norton & Company.

Weeks, G.R. & Treat, S.R. (2001). *Couples in treatment: Techniques and approaches for effective practice* (2nd ed.). Philadelphia: Brunner-Routledge.

Wheeler, G. (1994). The tasks of Intimacy: Reflections on a gestalt approach to working with couples. In G. Wheeler and S. Backman (Eds.), *On intimate ground: A gestalt approach to working with couples* (pp. 31–59). San Francisco: Jossey-Bass.

Wile, D. (2011). Collaborative couple therapy: Turning fights into intimate conversations. In D.K. Carson & M. Casado-Kehoe (Eds.), *Case studies in couples therapy* (pp. 303–316). New York: Routledge.

Zilbergeld, B. (1995). The critical and demanding partner in sex therapy. In. R.C. Rosen & S.R. Lieblum (Eds.), *Case studies in sex therapy* (pp. 311–330). New York: Guilford Press.

Zilbergeld, B. (1999). *The new male sexuality.* New York: Bantam Books.

Zinker, J.C. (1994). *In search of good form: Gestalt therapy with couples and families.* San Francisco: Jossey-Bass.

INDEX